BASKETBALL MADE SIMPLE: A SPECTATOR'S GUIDE

THIRD EDITION

by P.J. Harari and Dave Ominsky

Illustrated by Stephen J. Lattimer
Cover design by Eugene Cheltenham
Hand signals by Anna Mendoza

Photographs © by
Allsport Photography and Bruce Bennett Studios

http://www.firstbasesports.com

Look for these other Spectator Guides:
- Football Made Simple
- Ice Hockey Made Simple
- Soccer Made Simple

Also published by First Base Sports:
- How to Win a Sports Scholarship

ISBN 1-884309-13-5
Library of Congress Catalog Card Number: 2002091854

We welcome your comments and questions:
FIRST BASE SPORTS, INC.
P.O. BOX 1731
MANHATTAN BEACH, CALIFORNIA 90267-1731
(310) 318-3006

Typesetting by Jelico Graphics

Special thanks to Karen Perez for her artistic assistance

HOW TO USE THIS BOOK

Basketball is played more than any other American team sport — not only in 99% of U.S. high schools and colleges but also in over 200 countries by children on city playgrounds and adults in gymnasiums. The grace and strength of the top collegiate and professional players helps fuel this popularity and creates millions of new fans every year. To them, basketball seems a simple game, yet understanding its rich subtleties is not that easy.

This book aims to educate anyone who wants to know more about this exciting international game. It is written for use by a variety of audiences — adults who want to become fans, children who want to learn the basics of the sport they are playing and even existing fans who want a quick reference guide to their favorite sport.

Each chapter has been written to stand alone, so you do not have to sit and read the book from cover to cover. However, the chapters do build on each other, so if you start at page 1 and read through to the end, the chapters flow logically and become more detailed as you progress.

This book will mainly discuss the rules of basketball as played at the professional level in the United States by both men and women. However, this book will also outline the differences in the rules used at the college level where they are important. Note that the same college rules generally apply to both men and women.

Rules, as well as any word or phrase printed in *italics*, can be referenced quickly and easily using the book's glossary or index. So get ready to learn about basketball — the team sport played by more Americans than any other.

BASKETBALL ORGANIZATIONS

National Basketball Association (NBA): The most popular professional league in the world was created by the merger of the *Basketball Association of America* and the *National Basketball League* in 1949. It currently has 29 teams, 1 of which is in Canada. More than 2.5 billion people worldwide can watch the NBA, as it is televised in 210 countries in 43 languages. The NBA's headquarters are in New York.

National Collegiate Athletic Association (NCAA): This voluntary association of U.S. colleges establishes and administers rules and standards for their athletics. It first developed basketball rules in 1908. Since 1939 it has hosted a tournament of the best college teams that culminates in the *Final Four* and crowns an annual champion. Though it started with only 8 teams, the field for this tournament has grown to 64 today. Its headquarters are in Indianapolis, Indiana.

Women's National Basketball Association (WNBA): Inaugurated in 1997, this 16-team league (8 original and 8 *expansion* teams added 1998-2000) plays from June through August. The league uses a smaller ball than the NBA and a combination of NCAA and NBA rules. The WNBA is headquartered in New York.

American Basketball League (ABL): Started in 1996, this women's league merged into the WNBA in December 1998.

Continental Basketball Association (CBA): Started in 1979, it was the only developmental league for the NBA through 1999. Former NBA star Isiah Thomas purchased this minor league in 1999 for $9 million, eliminated team owners and aspired to grow from 10 to 20 teams, but the league's value plummeted when the NBA decided to operate its own developmental league instead. In 2000, the NBA ordered him to sell the CBA before becoming the Indiana Pacers' head *coach*, but financial difficulties made it difficult to find a buyer and many blamed Thomas for the league's troubles. After a brief suspension of play in 2001, Thomas sold the teams back to their local owners. The revamped CBA with 8 surviving teams moved its headquarters from Phoenix, Arizona to Boise, Idaho. It plays a 56-game season from November through March followed by *playoffs* in April.

National Basketball Development League (NBDL): The NBA's new minor league began in 2001-02 with 8 teams that play a 56-game regular season from November to March followed by playoffs. Since these teams do not have a direct affiliation with specific NBA teams, its players (who must be at least 20 years old) may be "called up" to play for any NBA team. The league also provides training for non-players interested in working with the NBA, including management, operations and sales personnel.

Other minor leagues: In addition to the *NBDL* and *CBA*, the following minor leagues also play in the U.S. (abbreviation, # of teams, season): *American Basketball Association* (ABA, 8, November-April), *Eastern Basketball Alliance* (EBA, 7, January-April), *National Rookie League* (NRL, 5, June-August), *Southwest Basketball League* (SBL, 5, March-April) and *United States Basketball League* (USBL, 10, April-June).

USA Basketball: Organized in 1974 as the *Amateur Basketball Association of the USA (ABAUSA)*, this governing body for men's and women's basketball in the U.S. is responsible for selecting and training the national teams for worldwide competitions (e.g., the Olympics, Pan American Games, World University Games). It is actually an association made up of many other associations. In 1989, when *FIBA* modified its rules to allow professional players to participate in international competitions, this organization admitted the NBA as a member and changed its name.

Federation Internationale de Basketball Association (FIBA): The governing body of international basketball was founded in 1932 and today has 211 member nations. FIBA oversees Olympic competition and every 4 years stages a 16-nation *World Cup*.

Foreign leagues: Over 1,500 Americans are playing abroad on every continent, although the most competitive leagues are in Europe.

TABLE OF CONTENTS

ORIGINS & HISTORY OF BASKETBALL

Basketball is the only competitive team sport that completely originated in the United States. It started in Springfield, Massachusetts in 1891 when a young Canadian, *James A. Naismith* (See **Fig. 1**), while studying for the Presbyterian ministry, enrolled at the YMCA Training School because he wanted to do more than preach. The students there, who were studying to be YMCA athletic directors and secretaries, so disliked calisthenics that the head of the athletic department asked Dr. Naismith to devise an indoor game to replace these and fill the void between the football and baseball seasons.

Dr. Naismith's original basketball game employed 2 wooden peach baskets nailed to the boards of the gymnasium, 13 rules (5 of which still govern the game today) and 9 members on each team (simply because he had 18 students in his class). He was inspired by football, rugby, soccer, water polo, field hockey and lacrosse in creating his new sport although his rules stressed less contact than some of these sports. By placing the basket high up, he hoped to create a game of skill rather than power and size. (In fact, as the rules evolved over the years, many attempts were made to curb the advantages of height — but each time larger players adapted by increasing their range of skills.) When players grew tired of climbing with a ladder to reclaim the ball after every goal, the bottom of the basket was removed.

The game became an instant success as people across the country requested copies of the rules. Within three years it was introduced in Canada, Europe and as far as Australia, China and India, and rules were printed in 30 languages. During those early years the game was often rough and dangerous. To protect spectators from players

Fig. 1: Dr. Naismith holding his peach basket.

chasing the ball into the stands, a wire cage was built around the court — which is the reason basketball is still sometimes referred to as the cage game. The players would get cut from being thrown against the wires and the *court* was often covered with blood. Teams used only *layups* and 2-handed *set shots* to score before crowds of raucous fans.

That success did not last long, however. By the turn of the century, basketball fell into disrepute as it became even rougher. Also, gymnasiums that could otherwise be used by as many as 60 people at a time doing a variety of things were increasingly tied up with basketball games of only 18 players, limiting the gyms' availability to the general public.

This situation actually spurred the start of the professional game in the U.S. Players were forced to rent dance halls, skating rinks and other spacious locations to accommodate their game. They began charging admission to cover the rental fees and split any profits. Games at these unusual sites were often played around obstacles, such as pillars or posts. Opponents could be forced into these for a "post" play — a term still used to describe when a player acts as a pillar (or *screen)* for a teammate in the *post*.

However, these early leagues lacked stability and were often short-lived. The most well-known team in the 1920s was the *Original Celtics* who traveled from city to city beating the best teams. When the professional *American Basketball League (ABL)* was formed with 9 teams in 1925, the Celtics reluctantly joined and fans grew bored as the Celtics won nearly every game. The first all-black team, the *Rens* (formed because they were not permitted to join the early leagues), came on the scene around the same time, and a few years later a team of black basketball entertainers, the *Harlem Globetrotters*, also began touring the country.

Outside the U.S., basketball's popularity did not truly blossom until the late 1930s, when the sport was added to the 1936 Olympic Games and as U.S. servicemen stationed on foreign soil provided instruction abroad. Meanwhile, in the U.S., the leagues were in a state of disarray by 1930, following the economic setback of the Depression and waning interest. Basketball was kept alive at home by the more than 50 colleges that continued to play the game.

The sport's biggest strides came during the next 10 years due to 5 main factors: the building of large arenas, the introduction of big-time college basketball at Madison Square Garden (which brought about the creation of standardized rules and officiating), the introduction of a high-scoring version of the game, the acceptance of the one-handed shot, and annual tournaments (such as the *NIT* introduced in 1938 and the *NCAA* in 1939) which provided a goal for the country's best college teams.

The success of the college game encouraged the founding of the professional *National Basketball League* (*NBL*) in 1937 with 13 teams and the corporate sponsor support of Goodyear, Firestone and General Electric. However, the advent of World War II halted the new league's progress. It was not until 1946 that Walter A. Brown, president of Boston Garden, organized the first truly ordered pro league, the *Basketball Association of America* (*BAA*). In 1949 it merged with the remains of the NBL to form the *National Basketball Association* (*NBA*) which still exists today. A rival league, the *American Basketball Association* (*ABA*) was founded in 1967, but folded in 1976 merging some teams into the NBA.

It was in the 1970s that basketball's popularity exploded. By 1977, over 100 million spectators were attending organized basketball games at the high school, college and professional levels in the U.S. each year. The frequency of televised college games spurred on this growing interest. Today, the NCAA's *Final Four* tournament is one of the nation's major sporting events, rivaling the Super Bowl and World Series in number of viewers — over 136 million watched some part of the 2002 tournament.

Women were involved with basketball from the start. It was first played by the teachers at the Buckingham School in Springfield (including Maude Sherman, who would become Dr. Naismith's wife), but it was truly pioneered by Smith College which introduced the game in 1892. The first rules for women were written by Clara Baer of Newcomb College (New Orleans) in 1895. In the 1990s two professional leagues formed in the U.S.: *The American Basketball League* (*ABL*), inaugurated in 1996, which later merged into the *Women's National Basketball Association* (*WNBA*), founded in 1997.

What started as a slow, non-contact sport in Dr. Naismith's mind has evolved into a modern-day game of speed, grace, power and tremendous skill.

OBJECT OF BASKETBALL

Basketball is a fast-paced game played by 2 teams of 5 players each. The object is to toss a *ball* into the opposing team's *basket* to score *points* while preventing the opponent from doing the same. The team that scores the most points is the winner.

Although the game is usually played indoors, it can also be played on outdoor playgrounds, in garage driveways or anywhere else a basket can be set up. The fact that it can be played inside or out creates a year-round sport. Also, since the game requires no other equipment besides a ball and a basket, its easy set-up makes it equally popular among players of all ages in cities, suburbs and countrysides around the world.

Basketball's rules are continually evolving with an eye toward preserving a game of skill rather than brute force, in keeping with the original intentions of its creator, *Dr. Naismith*. These rules are also designed to keep the game moving while protecting players from injury — no small feat when so many large players vie for control of a ball in a rather small area.

Basketball may seem to be such a simple game, yet there are important rules and strategies you can learn that will make it more fun to watch. With this notion in mind and the help of this book — which covers the rules and strategies of the professional and college game in the U.S. — you should be able to understand nuances of basketball you never noticed before, and enjoy it that much more.

THE BASKETBALL COURT

An indoor regulation basketball *court* has a hardwood surface and is rectangular in shape. Its maximum dimensions are 94 x 50 feet and there is no rule that specifies how small a court may be. It is common today for arenas to have the home team's logo painted onto the hardwood surface.

The court's boundaries are called *sidelines* along its length and *end lines* (or *baselines*) along its width. (See **Fig. 3** on the next page) When a player with the ball (or the ball itself) touches any part of these lines or the area outside of them, he is considered *out of bounds* and his team loses *possession* of the ball. (See **Fig. 2**) Sometimes players make acrobatic mid-air attempts to retrieve a ball heading out of bounds and throw it back *inbounds* before either they or the ball touch the ground out of bounds.

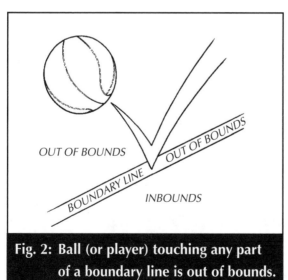

OUT OF BOUNDS

OUT OF BOUNDS

BOUNDARY LINE

INBOUNDS

Fig. 2: Ball (or player) touching any part of a boundary line is out of bounds.

Basket, Rim and Backboard
At each end of the court a *basket* is attached to the lower center of a *backboard* generally made of transparent plexiglass

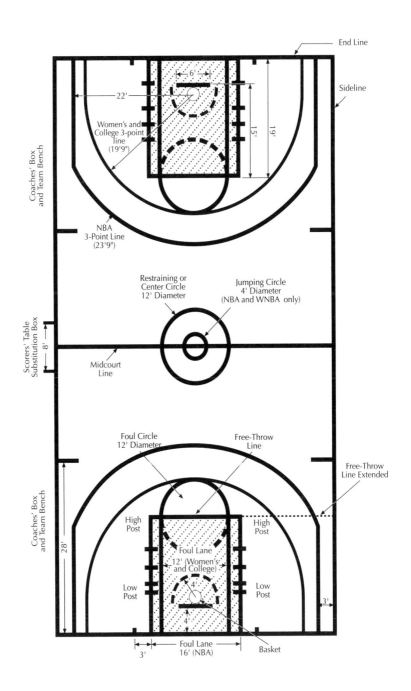

End Line

Sideline

6'

22'

Women's and
College 3-point
line
(19'9")

15'

19'

Coaches' Box
and Team Bench

NBA
3-Point Line
(23'9")

Restraining or
Center Circle
12' Diameter

Jumping Circle
4' Diameter
(NBA and WNBA only)

Scorers' Table
Substitution Box

8'

Midcourt
Line

Foul Circle
12' Diameter

Free-Throw
Line

Free-Throw
Line Extended

High
Post

High
Post

Coaches' Box
and Team Bench

28'

Foul Lane
12' (Women's
and College)

Low
Post

4'

Low
Post

3'

4'

3'

Foul Lane
16' (NBA)

Basket

Fig. 3: A basketball court.

6

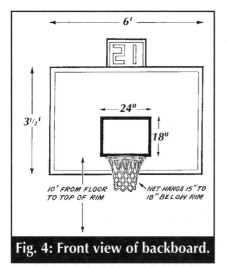

Fig. 4: Front view of backboard.

(See **Fig. 4**). Each basket consists of a horizontal metal ring 18" in diameter called the *rim* placed 10 feet above the court's surface with a bottomless *net* 15"-18" in length hanging from it. A small white rectangle is painted on the backboard above the rim to provide a target area for shooting the ball. A *shot clock* with big red numbers is also visible above each basket. In college, it is sometimes located on the floor just outside the corner of the court. A red light is also placed behind the backboard to signal the end of each *period*.

Each backboard is suspended 4 feet inside the end line, by a base located out of bounds. (See **Fig. 5**) This allows players room to maneuver behind the basket without going out of bounds. The base is padded to protect players who might accidentally collide with it. Some college arenas have backboards suspended from the ceiling for easier maintenance and to offer fans an unobstructed view of the game.

An interesting sidenote on backboards: they were once made of wood and metal (still used in high schools and gymnasiums), but were changed to glass to allow spectators to see through them. Today, plexiglass is used because it does not shatter as easily during play, and if it does, its falling pieces are less dangerous. While this used to be a rare occurrence, the advent of bigger and more athletic players is making this a more common problem. In fact, the *NBA* now requires each arena to have an extra backboard unit on the premises during games to prevent costly delays if a backboard shatters.

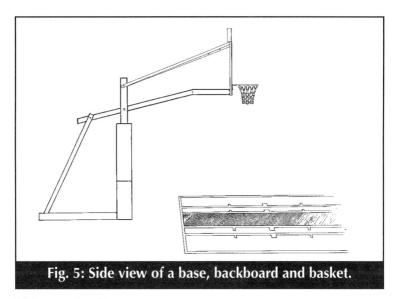

Fig. 5: Side view of a base, backboard and basket.

Lines on the Court

Dividing the Court — The *center* or *midcourt line* runs parallel to the end lines and divides the court into two halves called the *frontcourt* and the *backcourt*. The frontcourt contains the basket at which Team A is shooting to score points; the backcourt is the area Team A is defending (where Team A is trying to stop Team B from scoring). Only the team on offense has a frontcourt and backcourt. When Team B becomes the offense, its frontcourt is where Team A's backcourt used to be.

In addition to the midcourt line, several other important lines are painted on the court's surface:

Center Circle — At the center of the court are 2 circles which are used for *jump balls* including the one that starts the game. One is 4 feet in diameter (the *jumping circle* —NBA and *WNBA* only) surrounded by another 12 feet in diameter (the *restraining circle*), and together they are called the center circle. Two other 12-foot *foul circles*, located one at each end of the court, are also used for jump balls.

Foul Line (or *Free-Throw Line*) — a line 16' long (12' in college and for women) located 15' away from the backboard from which players take unobstructed shots at the basket (called *free-throws* or *foul shots*) after a *foul* is committed by the opposing team.

Foul Lane — an area 19' long and 16' wide (12' in college and for women), bordered by the end line and the foul line. Players must stand with both feet outside this lane area during a free-throw. Also, players lingering too long in this area during play may be called for a *3-second violation*. The entire foul lane is painted a different color than the rest of the court. A player standing in it is said to be *in the paint*.

The *Key* — At each end of the court is a key (named for the keyhole shape this area had many years ago). The 3 elements of the key are the foul circle, the foul lane and the free-throw line.

3-Point Line — In each half of the court is drawn a large horseshoe-shaped line called the 3-point line. Players who shoot the ball into the basket while standing with both feet completely behind this line (or one foot, if the other is in mid-air) earn 3 points — the maximum for any single shot. In the NBA, this line is an arc 23'9" from the basket intersecting parallel lines drawn from the baseline, each 22' from the basket. The NBA experimented with an arc 22' from the basket from 1995-97 but moved it backwards when the shot proved too easy to make. It is 19'9" in college and for women, with a slightly different shape.

Areas Located Out of Bounds — Various hash marks are also drawn along the sidelines. These designate, among other things, the 8 foot *substitution box* in front of the *scorers' table* where players wait to enter the game, and the *coaches' boxes*, the area beyond which the coaches cannot roam during play. Along the same side of the court are 2 benches (or chairs) where the players, coaches and trainers from each team sit during the game. Separating these 2 benches is the scorers' table, where the *scorers* and *timekeepers* sit.

Now let us see what **UNIFORMS & EQUIPMENT** players use.

UNIFORMS & EQUIPMENT

Much of basketball's popularity can be attributed to its simple needs in player and *court* equipment. It is easy for any player with a pair of athletic shoes to find a simple *rim* attached to a wall or pole to practice *shooting*. All he needs is one other friend to play a game of *one-on-one*. Basketball is an inexpensive sport whose set-up is readily available everywhere in the world.

Professional basketball players wear simple *uniforms* — shorts and sleeveless jerseys adorned with their team's logo. During games, the home team wears light-colored uniforms and visitors wear darker-colored ones. A player's number is printed at least 6" high on both sides of the jersey, and his name appears on the back. Today, college players often wear a T-shirt underneath their jersey (illegal in the *NBA*), and the shorts seem to get longer every season. A few players even wear 2 pairs of shorts, with a longer pair beneath the official trunks (a style readily mimicked by American kids), although the NBA now requires the hem of its players' shorts to be at least 1 inch above the knee.

The sneakers worn by players are called high-tops, designed to support and protect the ankles. This is the only part of the NBA uniform on which commercial logos may be worn. New designs with innovative features are continually introduced by the biggest athletic shoe companies, such as shoes with air pumps. These are highly coveted by youngsters who try to emulate the star athletes. One famous TV ad claimed (tongue-in-cheek) "it was the shoes" that gave *Michael Jordan* his incredible leaping ability.

The equipment is also simple — a *ball* and a *basket*. The ball itself is an inflated sphere made of an airtight rubber casing covered with leather that is about 30 inches in circumference (29" college and *WNBA*) and weighs about 22 ounces. It is inflated to $7\frac{1}{2}$ - $8\frac{1}{2}$ pounds of pressure.

Now let us see how *points* are scored using this ball.

SCORING

There are 2 ways to score in basketball: a *field goal* or a *free-throw*. A field goal is scored anytime the ball comes down through the top of the *basket* during play. It counts for 2 *points*, unless it is thrown by a player with both feet completely behind the *3-point line* (or at least one foot if the other is in mid-air), where it counts as a *3-point shot*. *Inside shooting* occurs near the basket, usually in the *key*, while *outside* (*perimeter*) *shooting* occurs from outside the key, near or beyond the 3-point line.

A free-throw is a shot taken from the *foul line* by a player who is un*guard*ed. Each successful free-throw counts for 1 point. One or 2 free-throws are taken when a player "goes to the line" depending on the situation that brought him there (discussed in the chapter on **VIOLATIONS & FOULS**). Players who are fouled in the process of shooting a 3-point shot get 3 free-throws (though prior to 1995 only 2 were awarded in the *NBA*).

Free-throws are generally easier to make because the shooter is not distracted by any opponents and he can take up to 10 seconds in preparing his shot. Around 20% of the points in an NBA game come from free-throws, so all players practice free-throws extensively. A team with a good *free-throw percentage* has a big advantage, not only because so many free-throw opportunities present themselves during a game but because intentional fouls in the final minutes of close games put players in foul-shooting situations.

When a player scores a 2-point field goal and is fouled in the process, he goes to the line for a single free-throw to try to complete a *3-point play*. (Be sure not to confuse this with the 3-point shot mentioned above.) The 3-point play generally gets the fans very excited. Even more exciting, but rarer, is the *4-point play* where a player is fouled as he is shooting a successful 3-point shot, and then makes the free-throw for a total of 4 points.

Fig. 6: Standard free-throw set-up.

During the free-throw, players from both teams stand along either side of the *foul lane* to *rebound* any final free-throw that is missed, making sure not to step into the lane until the shooter *releases* the ball. (See **Fig. 6**) Players from both teams (up to 6 in college, but only up to 5 in the NBA), line up in alternating order, starting with the non-shooting team closest to the basket. Those players not lining up along the lane must stand behind the *3-point line* (and the *free-throw line extended* in college). A player who steps into the lane early or distracts the shooter commits a *free-throw lane violation.*

For a *technical* free-throw, only the shooter goes to the line. All the other players are required to stand behind him to limit potential distraction.

Basketball is a game of streaks with teams gaining momentum and often scoring several times in a row. When such a *run* occurs an announcer will point it out by saying, for example, "The Lakers are on a 10-2 run." This means that the Lakers scored 10 points while their opponents scored only 2 in the same period of time. For the Lakers to have scored 8 more points, their opponents must have missed several shots or committed *turnovers.*

Now let us see **HOW THE GAME IS PLAYED**.

HOW THE GAME IS PLAYED

The version of basketball played by professionals, colleges and high schools pits 5 players on each of 2 teams against each other. Yet the game can be played by just 2 players in what is called a game of *one-on-one*, while many informal and tournament matches are set up for *3-on-3*. Many of the sport's greatest players even practice daily for hours by themselves, sharpening their offensive skills against a lone *backboard*. Here we will explore the basics of basketball.

LENGTH OF GAME

A *regulation* game in professional basketball is divided into 4 *quarters* (or *periods*) each 12 minutes in length. College and *WNBA* games consist of two 20-minute *halves*. A 15-minute *halftime* separates the first half from the second half. A brief 130-second break separates the 1st and 2nd, and the 3rd and 4th quarters. The *public address operator* will announce when there are only 2 minutes left in the game or any *overtime* period.

OVERTIME

When the score is *tied* at the end of a regulation game, additional 5-minute *overtime* (*OT*) periods are played until one team emerges victorious. One minute separates the end of a regulation college game from its overtime, 120 seconds in the WNBA and 130 seconds in the *NBA* (and between all subsequent OT periods). A *jump ball* is used to start each OT. As many OTs are played as are needed to break the tie. One college game between Bradley University and the University of Cincinnati in 1981 required 7 overtimes to decide the match in Cincinnati's favor. Teams do not switch sides for any of the overtimes needed, but continue to play on the sides assigned in the second half.

CHOOSING SIDES

A team's *basket* is the one it scores into (the one in its *frontcourt*). The visiting team always gets to choose which basket it wants to shoot at for the first half. Teams switch sides after the first half, and stay there for the second half and any overtime periods.

OFFENSE VS. DEFENSE

During the game, one team or the other will have control or *possession* of the ball. The team that gains possession is on *offense* and has the opportunity to score *points*. The other team becomes the *defense* and tries to stop the offense from scoring. Their fans will start yelling "DE-FENSE" during a game to urge them to stop the offense. Both defensive and offensive players combine speed, grace, power and endurance to play the game. The specialized skills that must be developed to succeed in competitive basketball are discussed in greater detail in the chapter on **PLAYER SKILLS**.

During the action, when the ball is not controlled by either team it is called a *loose ball* and neither team is offense or defense. You can tell a ball is loose when you see many players scrambling to get a hold of the ball. As soon as one team controls the ball, it becomes the offense.

Offense

The offensive players move the ball toward their own basket by bouncing it (called *dribbling*) or *passing* it among themselves to get a good shot and score. A player cannot run with the ball without dribbling it. The action is very rapid and may involve deceiving the defense to get by them. When a player with the ball moves very quickly toward the basket he is said to be *driving to the basket*.

Defense

The defense tries to prevent the offense from scoring by *guarding* it closely to force it to take difficult shots, by *blocking* these shots and by taking the ball away (called *steals*). When the offense loses possession through its own fault, it is called a *turnover* (although it is often a good defensive effort that throws the offense off-balance). Turnovers generally occur when the offense commits a foul or *floor violation* or makes a bad pass that is intercepted or goes *out of bounds*. A team that commits too many turnovers will often lose the game. It is easy to see how poorly a team is handling the ball when analysts list the number of turnovers each team has during the game.

14

THE JUMP BALL
Starting the Game

Any two players (usually the tallest players on the floor), one from each team, start the game by jumping for a ball that an official tosses above them. For the initial jump ball (or the *tip-off*) each jumper must stand with both feet inside the *restraining circle* (called the *center circle* in college). In the NBA and WNBA, each jumper must also have at least one foot on or inside the part of the smaller jumping circle in his own *backcourt* (See **Fig. 7**). The other players must stand with both feet completely outside the restraining circle (center circle in college) until one of the jumpers touches the ball.

The *official* then tosses the ball high above the heads of the jumpers and evenly between them. The jumpers cannot touch the ball until it has reached its highest point, so they actually tap it on its way down. One of the 2 jumpers must touch it before it reaches the floor or the official provides a new toss. Neither jumper can tap the ball more than twice or catch the ball himself. Also they must both stay completely inside the restraining circle until the ball has been tapped at least once.

Each jumper's goal is to tap the ball to one of his 4 teammates who try to gain possession of the ball, become the offense and try to score points. Players standing in the half of the court nearest their basket have first choice of position, although teammates cannot stand next to each other if an opponent wants to stand between them. In the NBA, if Team A wins the initial jump ball, Team B gets the ball to start the 2nd and 3rd quarters, while Team A starts the 4th. The WNBA begins each half with a jump ball. In college, the team with the *possession arrow* in its favor at the end of the first half gets the ball at midcourt to start the second half but a jump ball is used to start any overtime period.

Other Jump Ball Situations

In the NBA and WNBA, jump balls are also used in certain situations other than for starting a period. The most common

15

Fig. 7: Initial jump ball at center circle.

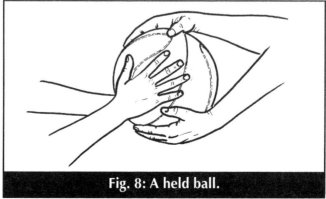

Fig. 8: A held ball.

of these is when 2 opponents hold the ball simultaneously so that both have possession. This is called a *held ball* (See **Fig. 8**), and "tying up the ball" is frequently done on purpose when both teams are competing for a loose ball. To restart the action an official makes the 2 players that held the ball jump. If a shorter player must jump against a taller player (a *mismatch*) he will be at a disadvantage. However, just stopping the action and flow of the game can provide important strategic benefits to a team.

Other jump ball situations include when:
- a ball that went *out of bounds* was last touched by both teams simultaneously
- officials are unsure/disagree over which of 2 opposing players last touched a ball before it went out of bounds
- simultaneous *personal fouls* are committed by 2 opponents during a loose ball
- *double fouls* result from disagreement among officials
- a ball becomes *dead* during play through neither team's fault
- a ball becomes lodged between the basket and backboard
- starting any overtime period (also applies to college)
- there is an inadvertent whistle by the officials

In all except the first 2 cases listed above, each team selects its best jumper (usually its tallest player on the floor) to take the jump at the center circle — just as they did for the tip-off. In the first two cases, the 2 players involved in the incident automatically become the designated jumpers — no matter what their size — at the circle closest to where the situation developed.

Possession Arrow
In college games, a *possession arrow* replaces the jump ball in the situations listed above to determine whose turn it is to throw the ball *inbounds*. The possession arrow is located near the *scorers' table*. After one team wins the tip-off, the arrow is set to give the other team possession after the next jump ball situation. The arrow changes on each subsequent jump ball situation, alternating which team gets possession

for the *throw-in*. This is why it is also called the *alternating-possession rule*.

STOPPING PLAY
Play stops in basketball every time there is a *dead* ball. Play is resumed by either a jump ball, a throw-in or a free-throw. The ball is considered dead in many situations, such as:

- when a *floor violation*, personal foul or *fighting* foul is called
- after the first of multiple free-throws is taken
- after a successful field goal or final free-throw
- when time expires at the end of any period (a successful field goal counts if the ball leaves a shooter's hands before the buzzer sounds)
- when there is a held ball
- when the ball rests on the rim, gets lodged between basket and backboard, or goes directly behind the backboard (See **Fig. 9**)
- after a technical free-throw is taken
- after any whistle by an official

RESTARTING PLAY
Live Ball
A ball is considered *live* as soon as it is given to the free-throw shooter, the thrower on a throw-in or when it is tossed up by the official on a jump ball. It becomes *alive* only when it is released by a shooter or thrower, or legally tapped by a jumper. The clock starts only when the ball becomes alive.

Fig. 9: A ball is dead if it goes directly behind the backboard.

Throw-in
After certain violations or fouls occur, the non-offending team will restart the game by throwing in the ball from a spot designated by

an official. For the throw-in, one player stands out-of-bounds at this spot and throws the ball to a teammate standing in bounds. (See **Fig. 10**) The thrower cannot hand the ball to the other player, throw it directly into the basket or bounce it out of bounds, and he must get it to someone within 5 seconds or his team loses possession. A throw in from the midcourt line into the backcourt is permitted any time in college, but in the NBA only in the last 2 minutes of

Fig. 10: Throw-in.

regulation, or in overtime. The defense tries to prevent the thrower from getting the ball inbounds, especially toward the end of close games. A defender may not slap at the ball or knock it out of the thrower's hands, and he must allow the thrower room to maneuver. If the offense is unable to complete the throw-in in time, it loses possession unless it uses a precious *timeout*.

THE CLOCKS

Time is very important in basketball. It affects almost everything players do — from how long players stand in one place, to how fast they try to get to a certain location, to the speed with which they must get a shot off.

Official Game Clock

The *official game clock* counts backwards to show how much time is left in each period (for example, if this clock says 5:31, that means 5 minutes and 31 seconds remain in the period). During the last minute of each period, the time is given in tenth-of-a-second intervals (e.g., 10.6 seconds remaining). This clock starts when a jump ball is legally tapped by one of the jumpers, a throw-in is legally touched by any inbounds player, a missed final free-throw attempt is touched by any player, or whenever an official signals to the *timer*.

The clock is stopped when an official blows his whistle because of:
- a personal foul, technical foul or floor violation
- a jump ball situation
- a *timeout* request
- an *official's timeout* for an emergency
- an official's timeout for a TV commercial break
- a need to confer with the other officials
- an unusual delay
- during the last minute of the 1st, 2nd and 3rd periods (2nd half and any overtime in college) following every successful field goal (no whistle)
- during the last 2 minutes of regulation or any OT periods following a successful field goal (no whistle)(NBA only)
- to signal an alternating-possession situation (college only)

Shot Clock (or 24-Second Clock)

There is also a *shot clock* to limit the length of time a team with the ball has to shoot it. In the NBA, this limit is 24 seconds so the shot clock is more commonly called the *24-second clock*. In college, men use a *35-second* clock and women a *30-second clock*. The WNBA also uses a 30-second clock. The shot clocks are usually located above each basket at the top of the backboard clearly visible to all players. In college arenas they are sometimes located in the corners of the floor instead.

Like the game clock, it counts down, showing how much time remains (e.g., 6 means the offensive team has 6 seconds left before the shot clock expires). If the clock reaches 0 before the offense *releases* a shot that either hits the rim or scores, the offense is penalized for a *shot clock violation*, also called a *24-second violation* (or *35* or *30-second violation*) and loses possession. As soon as the ball hits the rim or there is a change of possession, the clock is reset.

However, if the defense knocks the ball out of bounds the offense retains possession and takes the throw-in, but no time is added to the shot clock — it simply continues to play with just the unexpired time. Sometimes the defense will intentionally interfere with an offensive play to cause a throw-in situation that leaves the offense with too little time to set up a good shot attempt.

The 24-second clock was created to prohibit one team from keeping the ball for several minutes to prevent its opponent from scoring. This used to be a common tactic when one team was ahead near the end of the game, and it made the last few minutes boring for spectators, causing attendance to lag. In 1954, the NBA decided to limit the time a team could hold the ball, but it was unsure what amount of time was fair. Danny Biasone, owner of the Syracuse Nationals, suggested a logical way to determine this. By dividing the average amount of time a basketball game took to play by the average number of shots taken in a game, he concluded a shot was taken approximately every 18 seconds. A few seconds were added and the 24-second clock was born.

There are several other reasons to keep track of time in basketball. The officials count off 8 seconds (10 in college) in their heads for a player to get the ball from his backcourt across the *midcourt line* and 5 seconds for a throw-in. They also make sure that no player spends more than 3 seconds in the *key*. These issues are discussed in the chapter on **VIOLATIONS AND FOULS.**

Restarting the Clocks
Whenever the game clock is stopped, so is the shot clock. The game and shot clocks start again when the ball touches any player on the floor after a throw-in. After a free-throw, the game clock starts after the throw-in if the shot went in, or as soon as any player touches the ball after a final free-throw is missed. However, the shot clock only restarts when one team clearly gains possession of the ball. This is why there are times when the game clock is running and the shot clock has not yet been reset.

TIMEOUTS
Each NBA team is given 8 opportunities per game to stop play – 6 *full timeouts* (100 seconds in length for *mandatory*

timeouts, 60 seconds for all others) plus one *20-second timeout* per half. Teams use the time to rest and discuss strategy with their *coaches* and teammates by their bench. A team cannot use more than 3 full timeouts in the fourth period, and cannot "call" more than 2 in the last 2 minutes of regulation play. Leftover timeouts do not carry into overtime; instead 3 new 60-second timeout opportunities are provided to each team for each overtime period, the only restriction being that a team may not call more than 2 in the last 2 minutes of the period.

A team is "charged" (uses one up) with a timeout every time it requests one or whenever an official assigns a mandatory timeout. There must be at least 2 full timeouts called in the 1st and 3rd quarters, and 3 in the 2nd and 4th quarters. In the 1st and 3rd periods, if neither team has taken one prior to 5:59 remaining, the official scorer will charge the home team with a mandatory timeout at the first dead ball. If neither team calls a second timeout prior to 2:59 remaining in the quarter, the scorer again charges a mandatory timeout, this time to the visiting team. In the 2nd and 4th quarters, if neither team has called a timeout prior to 8:59 left, the scorer will call a mandatory timeout that is charged to neither team. If no timeout is called by 5:59 and 2:59 remaining, the same rules apply as did in the 1st and 3rd quarters. No timeout is charged if a team questions an official's call and a correction is made.

After any timeout taken during the last 2 minutes of regulation or overtime (final minute in the WNBA), the offensive team has the option of taking its throw-in at midcourt instead of starting in the backcourt. This saves the time and risk of bringing the ball the length of the court.

In men's college basketball each team usually gets 4 full timeouts (75 seconds each) and two 30-second timeouts in a game, to be used at any time. During broadcast games (TV, radio or Internet) where at least 3 commercial timeouts are automatically provided (and not charged to either team), each team only gets one 60-second and four 30-second timeouts per game (only 3 of these 30-second timeouts may be carried over to the second half). In both broadcast and non-broadcast games, 1 additional timeout is given for each overtime period. Any timeouts not used in a period roll over into the next (including overtime).

Timeouts can only be requested by a player on the floor when his team has possession of the ball, when the ball is dead, when an injured or disqualified player is being replaced, or when play has been stopped by the officials to correct a scoring error. The official must acknowledge the player's request to stop play. Coaches can signal to their players that they want them to call a timeout and come to the sidelines to talk things over, but they cannot request the timeout themselves. Teams may also use a timeout to their advantage in certain key situations which are discussed in the chapter on **THINGS TO LOOK FOR DURING PLAY / STRATEGY** (e.g., to see how a team is set up on a throw-in, or to prevent a *5-second violation*).

In both college and pro games, if a player calls for a timeout when his team has none left, his team is assessed a *technical foul*. This can be a costly mistake for a player to make. During the championship game of the 1993 *NCAA Final Four*, *Chris Webber*, whose Michigan Wolverines were 2 points behind with 11 seconds left in the game, called for a timeout when his team had none left. A technical foul was called and the opponent, North Carolina, made both its foul shots and got the ball out of bounds, ultimately beating Michigan by a score of 77-71.

TIMEOUTS AND INJURIES
In the case of a serious *injury* or other emergency, college officials may use an *official timeout* to stop play and protect the player. In college, a timeout is not charged to the player's team if he is able to continue playing immediately, if he needs only to retrieve his glasses/contact lenses or if he is immediately *substituted* for. In the NBA, officials only interrupt play if a player is bleeding to allow the injured player's team either to immediately substitute another player into the game or to call a time out. Officials will generally

wait until the ball becomes dead or is in the control of the injured player's team before stopping play. This is to prevent a player from faking an injury to stop the opponent's momentum (e.g., *fast break* opportunity).

SUBSTITUTIONS

The first 5 players a team puts on the court are the *starting lineup*, usually consisting of its best players. Whenever a player needs to come out of the game, whether it is due to fatigue, injury, *foul trouble*, or the coach's desire to try a different approach, a substitute replaces him from the *bench*.

Any substitute must first report to the *scorers' table* to give his name and number, and that of the player he is replacing. He must then sit in the *substitution box* located in front of that table to wait for the next dead ball. He can only come onto the floor after the horn has blown and an official beckons him in. Substitutions can be made during timeouts and in between periods without waiting (except in college during the last 15 seconds of a timeout, or after successful field goals in the last minute of the game or any *overtime* period). Free-throw shooters and jumpers involved in a jump ball cannot be substituted for unless they are injured. In such a case, the coach of the opposing team selects the replacement player.

An NBA rule passed in response to concerns about *infection control* requires the officials to remove any player who is bleeding, no matter how minor the cut or wound. As soon as the official can stop play, this player is removed and a substitute is sent in immediately. Before stopping play, officials will wait until a bleeding player has taken his free-throws or competed for a jump ball, and they will not interrupt a fast break opportunity. The player's team may choose to take a timeout instead of sending a substitute in, especially if the bleeding player can be attended to quickly. As soon as the player's wound is dressed to prevent the contamination of others, he may return to the game.

Now that you have an understanding of the procedures used in running an organized basketball game, let us learn about the **PLAYER SKILLS** needed in competitive basketball.

PLAYER SKILLS

Basketball players utilize the most basic athletic skills: running, jumping and handling a ball. These must be combined to develop *offensive* skills (*dribbling, shooting, pivoting, faking* and *passing*), *defensive* skills (*guarding, blocking* and *stealing*), and general skills (*rebounding* and *screening*). Each of these is discussed more fully below.

OFFENSIVE TEAM SKILLS
Passing

A pass is when one player throws the ball to a teammate. In general, the purpose of passing is to move the ball to get around *defenders* and score. Specifically, passing is used to:
- start a play
- move the ball down the court and closer to the basket
- get the ball to an *open* player (without defenders nearby) who is better skilled and/or in a better position to score
- avoid losing the ball (*turnover*) to a persistent defender

Any pass is successful if it gets to a teammate (the *receiver*) without being stolen by the opponent and improves the offense's position. The best passers have good *court vision*, meaning they are able to anticipate how plays will develop and determine where a receiver will become open. Since his teammates are in constant motion, a passer needs to throw the ball where he thinks a receiver is headed, called *leading* the receiver. Accuracy is critical because an imprecise pass is more easily stolen by an opponent. Good passes reach receivers at waist level or in their hands if they are ready to shoot. When a receiver makes a basket immediately after a pass, the passer is credited with an *assist*.

The area where a pass travels between the passer and the receiver is called the "*passing lane*." An opposing player may step into the passing lane in an effort to cut off a pass and either deflect or steal the ball. To keep defenders off-balance, ball handlers use a variety of passes depending on the situation:

Chest Pass — this 2-handed pass is the most common and quickest, used when there is no obstacle between the passer and receiver (usually around the *perimeter*). The ball is held to the chest and released with a flick of the wrists towards the receiver's chest.

Bounce Pass — the ball is bounced about $^2/_3$ of the way to the receiver. (See **Fig. 11**) Although it takes longer than a chest pass, it is more effective in a crowd of defenders. There are 2 versions — the 2-handed type is a chest pass with a bounce, while the 1-handed version is used to get around a defender by extending the arm to one side and releasing the ball with a flick of the wrist.

Baseball Pass (*Outlet* or *Full-Court Pass*) — named because its motion resembles that of a baseball player throwing, this 1-handed pass is used to traverse the length of the court, usually after a *defensive rebound*. The ball is thrown from above and behind the passer's shoulder to a receiver near the opposite basket. Though this pass is difficult to control and easy to intercept, it is the best for distance and is effective in starting the *fast break*.

Fig. 11: A bounce pass.

Overhead Pass — this 2-handed pass is similar to the chest pass except the ball is held over and slightly behind the passer's head, then quickly tossed over a defender's reach. (See **Fig. 12**). It is used by a player to get the ball over a defender closely guarding him, to reach a teammate under the basket or to initiate the fast break.

Fig. 12: An overhead pass.

Flick Pass (Sidearm Pass) — this rapid 1-handed pass from shoulder height often follows a fake. Its quick motion is designed to get the ball through an obstacle.

Thread-the-Needle Pass — a type of flick pass where the ball is squeezed through a narrow gap between 2 or more defenders to a receiver usually positioned under the basket, much as thread would go through the eye of a needle.

Behind the Back Pass — though rarely used because it is risky, this 1-handed waist-level pass behind the passer's back to a nearby receiver often catches defenders by surprise.

Lob Pass — this high-arcing 2-handed pass is aimed over the head of a receiver in mid-stride so he does not have to stop on his way to the basket. Also used to reach a tall teammate under the basket.

Touch Pass (Tap or Bat Pass) — this difficult maneuver requiring good court vision occurs when a receiver, instead of catching a pass, merely deflects it with his fingertips to a more open teammate

27

While passing is an extremely important skill, it is not the only way a team can move the ball or get by a defender. Another method is by dribbling.

OFFENSIVE INDIVIDUAL SKILLS
Dribbling
Dribbling is used to move the ball down the court, evade a defender, *drive* to the basket or set up a play. A player with the ball <u>cannot</u> run or walk without dribbling it. Dribbling is simply when a player continuously bounces the ball on the floor using his fingers and fingertips. He can be running, walking or even standing still as he dribbles. A *dribble series* ends when the ball handler allows the ball to rest in both his hands, shoots, passes, loses the ball or stops bouncing it. When dribbling, players always look ahead to survey the floor, never down at the ball.

The ball handler needs to follow certain rules while dribbling or his opponent will be awarded possession of the ball. He must:

- use only 1 hand at a time (but he can alternate hands)
- dribble only 1 series at a time — he cannot start, stop and start (or it is called a *double dribble*)
- not use his palm to slap or carry the ball
- take only 1 step for each bounce of the ball, unless he is shooting a *layup* (though this rule is generally ignored by college and pro officials so as not to interrupt the flow of the game)

The ball handler must be careful to maintain control of the ball between bounces since defenders will be trying to steal the ball away. Fast dribbles close to the floor allow for greater ball control. High, slow dribbles are used to travel long distances down the court. A good dribbler is able to change the pace of his dribble to be less predictable and change hands (e.g., *crossover dribble*) or directions quickly. He can move the ball straight ahead, backwards, left, right, behind his back or between his legs.

Faking

Throughout a game, players are always trying to deceive their opponents into thinking they are going to do one thing when they actually do another. These are called *fakes* or *feints*. Any part of the body can be used, including the eyes, to confuse a defender. For example, a player can pretend to shoot but dribble by his opponent, pretend to pass in one direction then pass in another, take a step right and dribble left, and so on. A *head fake* is one of the most effective, where a player moves his head as if he is going to shoot the ball but does not shoot, causing a defender to jump too early. It is a constant challenge for opponents to keep up.

Shooting

Shooting is how teams score points and win games. Shooters need good hand-eye coordination to place the ball in the basket. However, *shot selection* is just as crucial. Players should only *release* their shot when they are in good shooting position (facing the basket or "squared up") and within their own personal "shooting range". A shooter's job is made more difficult because defenders try to *block* his shot (interfere with it by touching or "getting a piece of the ball" on its way to the basket). The best shooters are adept at faking, using their eyes, head and entire body to get clear of defenders. Shots that look erratic are often desperate last-second attempts before the *shot clock* runs out.

Good shooters propel the ball with the fingertips of one hand only, imparting a slight backspin to the ball. Most also shoot the ball high into the air with an arc, so it will go over the *rim* more easily. Players who are able to provide the right combination of spin and arc are said to have a "soft touch". Even inaccurate shots thrown with a soft touch may score if they bounce lightly off the rim and into the basket, called a "shooter's roll".

While players can be as creative as they like in shooting, some of the most common shots taken are:

Jump Shot — a player jumps up and shoots the ball while in mid-air. (See **Fig. 13**) Before his shot, the ball rests in the palm and fingers of his shooting hand and is supported by the other hand. It is then propelled by the fingertips in an arc toward the basket. He must release the ball before he lands or he is called for an *up-and-down violation*, a form of *traveling*. It is the most widely used shot, popular because it allows a player to shoot over taller defenders or to change his mind at the last minute and pass to a more open teammate (called a *jump pass*). The jump shot is especially effective when combined with a head fake, since a slight deceptive delay before jumping may cause a defender to jump too early. There are also turn-around jumpers which surprise the opposition. Today, players have increased the range of this shot up to 30 feet from the basket, making it an even more dangerous weapon.

Set Shot — same as the jump shot except it is taken from a standing position, with both feet firmly planted on the floor during the release, usually 20 feet or more from the basket. Today it is rarely used, but is still important since most *free-throws* are set shots.

Free-throw or *foul shot* — a set shot taken from the *foul line* with no one guarding the shooter. Players make a higher percentage of these than regular set shots because there are no defenders to distract them. The shooter can take up to 10 seconds to release the ball; often he bounces the ball several times, choosing where to place his hands on it before shooting. *Rick Barry*, one of the best free-throw shooters of all-time, used a 2-handed underhanded foul shot which is rarely used today. A team's free-throw shooting can greatly affect the outcome of the game (See the chapters on **SCORING** and **THINGS TO LOOK FOR DURING PLAY/STRATEGY** for more information.)

Layup (*Layin* or *Finger Roll*) — the shot with the greatest chance for success (the highest percentage shot). It is taken from very close range and *banked* off the *backboard* so it drops into the basket for a layup (or sometimes the ball is just dropped into the basket for a layin, though these terms are used interchangeably today). (See **Fig. 14**) Players usually take layups on the run ("off the dribble"), jumping off one foot to get the ball as close to the basket as possible. This shot is used whenever the shooter has a clear path to the basket and is commonly used to finish a *fast break*.

Reverse layup — one of several creative variations of the layup where a player drives toward the basket, passes under it and shoots the ball from the other side of the rim using either hand.

Hook Shot — one of the most difficult shots to make and to defend against, this is a favorite of players in the *low post* position. Both the basket and the defender are behind the shooter until he releases the ball. The ball is held chest high

Fig. 13: A jump shot.   Fig. 14: A

with both hands as the player pivots and extends one arm up in a sweeping motion toward the basket before releasing the ball. *Kareem Abdul-Jabbar* made famous a version of this dubbed the *skyhook*, a shot that was impossible to block since he was 7'2" tall.

Fig. 15: A slam dunk.

Dunk (*Slam dunk*, Jam or Stuff) — when a player in close proximity to the basket jumps and strongly throws the ball down into it (See **Fig. 15**). A player is only permitted to hang on the rim after dunking to prevent injury to himself or others. Dunks are often the most athletic and creative of shots (sometimes thrown backwards and over the head) and are a favorite of tall, physical players. The dunk is often used to intimidate opponents, or to "fire up" (instill excitement among) spectators and teammates experiencing a temporary slump. It is during this shot that a backboard may shatter. Banned in the college game from 1968-1976, the dunk's critics point to missed scoring opportunities when a "hotdogging" (showoff) player forgoes an easy layup for a dunk and then misses it.

Tip in — a one-handed deflection used mostly by tall players to redirect a rebound or an off-target shot by a teammate to the basket.

Alley-oop — an acrobatic play where a passer lobs the ball to a teammate who snags it in mid-air and dunks it in one motion. It requires an accurate pass and perfect timing.

Pivoting
A player holding the ball (either because he has just received a pass or has stopped dribbling,) is permitted to rotate in any direction with one stepping foot, as long any part of his other foot (called his *pivot* foot) remains touching the floor. This ability of a player to turn quickly on one foot is important in passing and shooting, and to prevent *traveling* violations. The pivot foot is always the first foot a player lands on while catching the ball, but if he lands on both feet simultaneously, he can choose which foot to swivel on.

Screening
A *screen* is set when an offensive player uses his body to create an obstacle for the defense to allow a teammate to get open or closer to the basket. A player setting a screen (also called a *pick*) must be stationary or a *blocking foul* is called against him. A defensive player needs to beware of the opposing team's screen because if he runs into it he may be called for a foul or lose the player he was guarding. This offensive player would then be free to receive a pass or drive to the basket.

CROSSOVER SKILLS: OFFENSIVE AND DEFENSIVE
Rebounding
Rebounding is the one skill that is used both on offense and on defense. A *rebound* is when a player recovers a missed shot at the basket. When a player rebounds a shot missed by a teammate, it is called an *offensive rebound*. If the same player who took the shot gets the rebound it is said that "he got his own rebound." When the shot was missed by a member of the opposing team, it is called a *defensive rebound*. It is easier to get defensive rebounds than offensive rebounds. The team that controls the rebounding very often wins the game. Players try to position their bodies between their opponents and the basket, called *boxing out*. The best rebounders are strong, tall and have good jumping ability, although any player who knows how to box out well can get rebounds. Just as important as these physical attributes are good timing and the ability to anticipate where the ball will go after it hits the backboard or rim.

DEFENSIVE INDIVIDUAL SKILLS

The goal of defenders is to prevent the offense from scoring and to create turnovers (See **HOW THE GAME IS PLAYED**).

<u>Guarding</u>

Defensive players *guard* opponents by following them around the court to prevent them from driving towards the basket, taking open shots or making easy passes to teammates. A defensive player uses quick footwork to keep his body between his opponent and the basket, and usually holds his hands up in the air to interfere with passes and shots. However, the defender may not use physical contact to impede the movement of an opponent unless he has already *established his position* (see *blocking* in **VIOLATIONS & FOULS** chapter). Although minor hand-to-body contact (called *handchecking*) is illegal, recent NBA rule changes meant to improve the flow of the game encourage officials to ignore it if it does not impede the ball handler's speed, quickness, balance or rhythm. (See **Fig. 16**)

Fig. 16: Handchecking a player.

Shot Blocking

Shot blocking is an attempt by a defensive player to stop an offensive player's shot attempt with his hand. (See **Fig. 17**) Any deflection of a shot, no matter how slight, usually sends it off its intended course, preventing a basket. However, if a defender swipes at the ball but instead hits his opponent's arm or otherwise touches his body, the defender could be called for a foul. The one exception to this is that a defender can legally touch a shooter's hand while it is on the ball because the hand is considered part of the ball. Good shot blockers have

Fig. 17: Shot block attempt.

long arms, strong jumping ability and good timing to meet a shooter in mid-air.

Steals

Whenever a defender gets the ball by intercepting a pass or dislodging a dribbled ball, it is called a steal. The best players at stealing anticipate the next offensive action and move rapidly to recover the ball. Since a steal happens so quickly, it often allows the player who has stolen the ball to get a head-start toward his own basket where he can likely score unopposed. In such a case, not only did the steal prevent the offense from scoring 2 points, but it resulted in 2 points for the team that was on defense. This is called a 4-point *turnaround* (or swing) (2+2=4).

We are now ready to examine some of the **PLAYER POSITIONS** that use these skills.

PLAYER POSITIONS

In organized basketball there are always 5 players on the *court* per team — generally 2 *forwards*, a *center* and 2 *guards*. *Pick-up* games can be played with less than 5 players to a side. The best basketball players today are well-versed in all the skills we just reviewed in the chapter on **PLAYER SKILLS**, yet each of the 5 main player positions require a different mix of these as well as distinct physical attributes. Each player generally guards an opponent that plays the same position. Since possession can change at any moment, all the players must be prepared to switch from offense to defense and back.

In addition to the *starting lineup* (the 5 *starters* who are generally also the team's best players) a team's *bench* (all its other players) is also important to its overall success. In the *NBA*, each team is allowed to have a maximum of 12 active players on its *roster* (11 for *WNBA*). Since injuries are common, a team may have less than 12 players to rotate in, so it is best served by having several strong *substitutes* for all positions. Although college teams are not limited in size, only 13 Division I scholarships are available for men's teams, 15 for women.

Each NBA team is permitted to have one player *captain* and up to 2 co-captains. The captain is the only player who can talk to an *official* during a *timeout*, and then only to discuss a rule interpretation. Players who question an official's judgment risk being called for a *technical foul* and it seems like they test the limits every chance they get. The captain acts on behalf of the *coach* who cannot be on the court. Today, coaches constantly talk to their players on the court, but at one time this was not permitted. Nat Holman, a coach at City College of N.Y. (*CCNY*) in the 1950s, actually learned to be a ventriloquist so when he threw his voice it seemed his players were getting suggestions from fans in the stands!

GUARDS

The guards (*ball handlers*) tend to be the smallest and fastest members of the team, and they lead the offense by handling the ball and calling the plays. They need to be excellent *dribblers* because they start almost every play in the *backcourt* and must successfully move the ball into the *frontcourt*. Since they play the furthest away from the basket (covering the middle and backcourt) they must also be great *passers* to get the ball to teammates who are closer, or they must develop good *outside shooting* skills. Most of the best *3-point shooters* are guards. Guards sometimes *rebound*, but not as often as forwards or centers.

There are 2 types of guards with different functions; both types are represented on the floor at a time:

Point Guard (Lead guard, Number 1 guard, *Playmaker*) — the best ball handler on the team, he controls the ball more than any of his teammates. As the extension of the team's coach, he makes decisions on the floor which generate the team's offense, taking advantage of his teammates' strengths to create *scoring opportunities*. To make these decisions, it is important for him to have good *court vision* (the ability to see the entire floor to determine the position of teammates and defenders) as he dribbles the ball down the court. He uses hand signals to communicate the chosen plays to his teammates. Teammates usually try to get the ball back to the point guard whenever the defense breaks up one of their offensive attempts so that he can set them up again.

Shooting Guard (Second Guard, Off Guard, Number 2 Guard) — he is usually a reliable *outside (perimeter) shooter* quick at penetrating the defense and *driving to the basket* to score. Generally the shooting guard is also a talented dribbler and ball handler, though not as gifted as the point guard. On some teams his position can also be played by a small forward (or *swing man*).

FORWARDS

The forwards are bigger than the guards but smaller than the center, and they are commonly the team's highest scorers. On both offense and defense they play near the corners of the court on either side of the basket, taking *jump shots*, driving to the basket and rebounding. A team's 2 forwards serve different functions — one is more of a roaming shooter and the other is more of a rebounder:

Small Forward (Quick Forward) — he is often the most versatile player on a team, combining the quickness, agility and ball-handling skills of a guard with the physical strength to jostle under the basket and score amid large defenders. His skills include solid shooting from both the perimeter and close range, the ability to drive to the basket, and rebounding on both ends of the court. He is also the third player to join the guards on a *fast break*, so he is pivotal in the *transition* game.

Power Forward (Big Forward, Strong Forward) — the less agile and swift of the forwards, he is often interchangeable with the center. This player uses his height and strength primarily for defense and rebounding at both ends of the court. Offensively, he scores by making shots from close to the basket, and he also sets *screens* to free up his teammates for shots. The best power forwards are effective in both the *low post* and *high post* (**Fig. 18**),

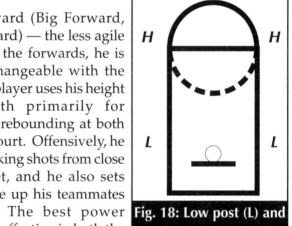

Fig. 18: Low post (L) and high post (H).

able to shoot while facing the basket or after receiving the ball with their backs to the basket (called *posting up*).

CENTER

The center (also called the *pivot* because many plays are created around him) is usually the tallest, biggest and strongest player on a team. Most professional male centers are 7' or taller, making them intimidating forces. Among his tasks, the traditional center lists rebounding, *blocking* shots and screening. Most centers are also adept at shooting close to the basket and from various angles, and may develop a *hook shot* from as far as 15' away which is very difficult to defend. Today's centers (especially some European players) have far greater skills than their counterparts did 10 years ago — they can run, dribble and even shoot from the outside.

Despite this increased versatility in modern day players, a center's primary position on the court is still closest to the basket, where he is able to *tip in* missed shots, receive passes from other teammates for easier shots at the basket, and rebound. It is important for him to have "good hands" (strong and reliable) to handle rebounds and passes. On occasion, a team will choose to replace the center, playing with 3 forwards/2 guards or 3 guards/2 forwards instead.

THE BENCH

The bench is a team's reserve, used by the coach to relieve his starters when they are tired or in *foul trouble*, or to change an offensive or defensive style of play. Since coaches put on the floor combinations of players who work well together, more than one substitution is often made at a time or in quick succession. The more talented substitute players a team has, the "deeper" is its bench. However, it is difficult to find players who are consistent coming off the bench because they enter the game "cold". A good substitute, however, must be able to get in the game and have an immediate impact, often for just a short period of time.

The best substitute on a team is called the *sixth man*. He is likely to be the first substitute brought into a game when the team needs a fresh player to do one or more of the following:
- change the pace of the game
- provide some offensive points
- throw off the opposition's offense with some over-powering defensive skills
- take control of the ball with strong rebounding

The behavior of all players is controlled by **THE OFFICIALS**.

THE OFFICIALS

Three *officials* control the conduct of a basketball game: a *crew chief* and 2 *referees*. College games use either 2 or 3: the referee and 1 or 2 *umpires*. They are all responsible for calling *fouls* and *violations*, indicating successful *field goals*, pointing to the location for *throw-ins* and inspecting all the equipment. Official *scorers* and *timers* assist them. All the officials have "elastic power" which is the authority to make immediate decisions on anything not specifically covered in the rules. Whenever officials are unsure about a decision, they confer with each other.

When a foul or violation occurs, the official who sees it blows his whistle to stop play and signals the timer to stop the *official game clock*. For *personal fouls*, the official also tells the scorer the offending player's *uniform* number, then puts up his fingers to show the number of *free-throws* to be taken. More of the signals officials use to communicate with each other and the players are illustrated in **OFFICIALS' HAND SIGNALS** at the end of the book.

CREW CHIEF
The head official in charge of a game is the crew chief, selected because he is the best and usually the most experienced official on the floor. Although the nearest official signals when a field goal is scored, it is the crew chief who makes the ultimate decision on whether or not a basket will count. He also decides all matters on which the other officials, scorers or timers disagree. In college games, the head official is the referee and he has similar duties to the crew chief, except he may not set aside or question another official's decision.

REFEREES AND UMPIRES
After the crew chief (referee in college), the second-ranking officials are the referees (umpires in college), who are generally the officials with the least experience.

SCOREKEEPERS

The scorer and his assistants sit at the *scorers' table*, located behind one of the sidelines, to keep the game's official scorebook. In this book, they record all *timeouts*, field goals made and missed, free-throws made and missed, and keep a summary of points scored. In addition to keeping count of all *team fouls*, they also record all personal and *technical fouls* called against each player and notify the officials when a player has 6 (5 in college) and needs to be removed from the game. To do their job, they keep track of the names, uniform numbers and positions of all the players in the game, and must be notified of the *starting lineup* and any *substitutions* made throughout the game. Every player that enters the game must first report to the scorers' table. The scorers provide summary score sheets to the media during the game and send a final game report to the league.

TIMERS

Two timers also sit at the scorers' table and record all playing time and stoppages in the game. One operates the official *game clock*, stopping it every time an official blows the whistle and restarting it when the official signals him to do so. The second timer operates the *shot clock*. A separate stopwatch is used during timeouts, called the timeout watch.

TELEVISION REPLAYS

College officials may use replay equipment or television monitors, but only to determine which individuals participated in a fight, to rectify a timer's or scorer's error, or to fix any problem relating to a malfunctioning of the clocks. They cannot rely on such outside sources for assistance in determining *goaltending*, *basket interference*, field goals, fouls or anything else except to resolve whether a field goal that will determine the outcome of the game (win, lose or tie) was shot before time expired. Although the NBA has never had a replay rule, starting in 2002-03 officials will be allowed to review last second shots at the end of each period to confirm whether they were *released* before time expired.

VIOLATIONS & FOULS

Basketball games are played in a relatively small area, especially when you consider the height and weight of the players involved. Each shot attempt concentrates most of these players into an even smaller space beneath the *basket*. As they battle for control of the *ball*, contact between them is frequent and often against the rules, so *officials* call only the most severe *fouls*. It is impossible for the officials to catch every violation, some infractions are difficult for them to detect (e.g., *palming*), and sometimes they even ignore incidental minor contact so the flow of the game is not disrupted.

There are 3 categories of violations or fouls: *floor violations*, *personal fouls* and *technical fouls*. When a player commits an infraction in handling the ball or by his position on the court, it is called a floor violation. Violations do not cause harm to any opponent nor do they prevent an opposing player's movement on the court. Personal fouls, on the other hand, are called for contact between players that may result in injury or which provides one team with an unfair advantage. All the personal fouls committed by members of a team are also counted collectively as *team fouls*. Technical fouls are called for some procedural violations and misconduct that officials believe are detrimental to the game.

When an official sees a foul or rule violation committed, he will blow his whistle to stop play and the *game clock* is stopped. He then identifies the foul or violation with a *hand signal* (See **OFFICIALS' HAND SIGNALS**) and enforces the penalty. The penalty for committing a foul or violation is to award the wronged team *free-throws* and/or the opportunity to throw the ball back *inbounds*. When a violation is committed by the offense, there is a change of *possession* as the defense inbounds the ball by a *throw-in*. If the violation was committed by the defense, the offense is either awarded free-throws or retains *possession* for the throw-in.

TABLE 1: SUMMARY OF PENALTIES

KEY: FT = Free-Throw; * = if the last FT is successful the opponent will throw in the ball

EVENT	NBA		College	
	Offensive	Defensive	Offensive	Defensive
Floor Violation	Throw-in by defense	Throw-in by offense	Throw-in by defense	Throw-in by offense
Shooting Foul	Not applicable	1 FT by offense if shot was successful* OR 2 FTs by offense if shot was unsuccessful* OR 3 FTs by offense if 3-point shot was unsuccessful*	Not applicable	1 FT by offense if shot was successful* OR 2 FTs by offense if shot was unsuccessful* OR 3 FTs by offense if 3-point shot was unsuccessful*
Non-Shooting Foul (Common Foul)	Throw-in by defense	If 4 or less team fouls per period: throw-in by offense. If over the limit (5 or more team fouls per period): 2 FTs by offense*	Throw-in by defense	If 6 or less team fouls per half: throw-in by offense. If over the limit (7 to 9 team fouls per half): 1-and-1 by offense (one FT plus a penalty)* OR If over the limit (10 or more team fouls per half): 2 FTs by offense*
Flagrant Foul	2 FTs and throw-in by defense	1 FT and throw-in by offense on a shooting foul where offense's shot was successful. 2 FTs and throw-in by offense if shot was unsuccessful or for fouls against a player without the ball	2 FTs and throw-in by defense	1 FT and throw-in by offense where offense's shot was successful. 2 FTs and throw-in by offense if shot was unsuccessful or for fouls against a player without the ball
Technical Foul	1 FT and throw-in by the team that had possession at time the technical was committed	1 FT and throw-in by the team that had possession at time the technical was committed	2 FTs and throw-in by defense	2 FTs and throw-in by offense
Away-From-the-Play Foul	1 FT and throw-in by defense	1 FT and throw-in by offense	Called a non-shooting foul	Called a non-shooting foul

Fig. 19: Throw-in locations (T) shown on half court.

PENALTIES

Table 1 summarizes the penalty for each violation or foul.

Throw-In

When an official determines that a violation or non-shooting foul occurred, the ball is considered *dead* and the wronged team restarts the game by throwing in the ball from the spot he designates. (See chapter on **HOW THE GAME IS PLAYED**). **Fig. 19** shows the various inbounding locations from which a throw-in can be taken.

Shooting Free-Throws

In certain instances, the commission of a foul by a team allows a player from the opposing team to go to the free-throw line. The number of free-throw opportunities awarded depends on the type of foul that was committed. When a player "in the act of shooting" is fouled, it is called a *shooting foul*. It does not matter if the shot had no chance of going into the basket or if the official blew his whistle before the ball left a shooter's hands. Since officials subjectively determine whether or not a player was in the act of shooting, ball handlers who see that they are about to be fouled often make a last second attempt to shoot just to "get to the line".

The following scenarios (summarized in **Table 1**) are possible:

- 1 free-throw: awarded when a shooting foul is committed on a player whose shot was successful. This sets up a potential *3-point play* (or the very rare *4-point play* if the successful basket was a *3-point shot*).
- 2 free-throws: awarded when a player is fouled while shooting and misses the shot. Also awarded for *non-shooting fouls* when the fouling team is *over the limit* in team fouls (discussed below).
- *1-and-1*: in college only, where the second free-throw (also called a *penalty* free throw) is only taken if the first attempt was successful. Also awarded for non-shooting fouls when the fouling team is *over the limit*.

- 1 or 2 free-throws <u>and</u> the ball out of bounds: awarded for a *flagrant foul* on any player (with or without the ball); 1 if the fouled player made his shot, 2 otherwise; the fouled team keeps possession of the ball after shooting the free-throw(s).
- 3 free-throws: awarded if a player is fouled in the act of shooting from behind the *3-point line.*
- 1 technical free-throw: awarded to a team for any technical foul committed by its opponents, it is taken by the team's best free-throw shooter on the court at the time the foul was committed. In college, 2 technical free-throws are taken by the non-offending team who also then gets possession.

VIOLATIONS

Through the 1950s, basketball games suffered from low scores because there were no rules to prevent one player from controlling the ball for long periods of time. Since fans quickly became bored with these tactics, rules were created to increase the pace of the game. The most common violations are discussed below in alphabetical order:

- *Backcourt Violation* (or *Over-and-Back*) — once the offense brings the ball into its *frontcourt*, it cannot go into the backcourt with it unless an opponent causes it to go there through a deflection or other interference. Sometimes a player gives up pursuing a *loose ball* that is rolling towards his backcourt because he knows even if he catches up to it, his team will lose possession of the ball for this violation. A throw-in from the *midcourt line* into the backcourt is permitted anytime in college, but in the *NBA* only in the last 2 minutes of *regulation*, or in *overtime.*

- *Double Dribble* — this type of *illegal dribble* is called when a dribbling player picks up or touches the ball with both hands simultaneously and then continues dribbling. A player may dribble for a second time if a *field goal* attempt touches the *rim* or *backboard* first, or if his first series of dribbles ended involuntarily (such as when an opponent touched the ball).

- *Eight-Second Violation* — from the moment the ball is touched by an inbounds player on the throw-in in the backcourt, the offensive team has only 8 seconds (10 in college or WNBA) to cross the *midcourt* line into the frontcourt. This rule was added in 1932 to increase the game's tempo, prevent stalling, decrease keepaway games and encourage full-court defense. The only exceptions to this rule are in the event of:
  - a kicked or punched ball by the defense
  - a technical foul or *delay of game* warning against the defense
  - suspension of play by an official for *infection control* (e.g., if a player is bleeding)

- *5-Second Back-to-the Basket* (NBA only) — a ball handler in his frontcourt cannot dribble with his back or side to the basket for more than 5 seconds once he crosses the *free-throw line extended*.

- *Five Seconds Violation* (college only) — occurs when a ball handler holds the ball for 5 seconds while an opponent is within 6 feet of him.

- *Free-Throw Lane Violation* — players lined up along the *foul lane* during a free-throw attempt may not step into the lane until the shooter has released the ball. If an offensive player steps in, the free-throw is forfeited and the defense gets the ball out of bounds; if a defensive player steps in, the free-throw counts if it was good or it is rethrown.

- *Illegal Assist in Scoring* — a player cannot use the rim or the backboard to lift himself up and score. Similarly, a player cannot assist another player in scoring by giving him extra height.

- *Kicked* or *Punched Ball* — a defensive player cannot intentionally kick, knee or punch a ball.

- Palming — a ball handler cannot dribble the ball by scooping or carrying it in his palm. Though often done by players, this type of illegal dribble is difficult to detect so officials rarely enforce it.

- *Swinging Elbows* — excessive or vigorous swinging of the elbows by a ball handler holding the ball near a defensive player is not permitted, even if there is no contact.

- *Ten-Second Violation* — see Eight-Second Violation above

- *Three-Second Violation, Defensive* — A defensive player must actively guard an opponent within 3 seconds of stepping into the foul lane (or the imaginary 4' area extending out of bounds from it behind the basket). The 3-second count stops when the defender begins to actively guard an opponent or steps out of the designated area, or when there is a *field goal attempt* or a *loose ball*. Only a single defender may guard the ball handler in this area, or the offensive team is awarded a *technical foul* — in other words, the *zone defense* can be played anywhere on the court in the NBA, except *in the paint*.

- *Three-Second Violation, Offensive* — No offensive player can stand in the *foul lane* (or the imaginary 4' area extending out of bounds from it behind the basket) for more than 3 seconds. A player in the act of shooting can, however, finish his shot even if the 3 seconds expires. The count starts only when the ball is in the offense's frontcourt. A player can step out of the *key* and back in to give himself a new 3-second count. This rule prevents offensive players from stationing themselves below the basket waiting for a pass and an easy scoring opportunity, and forces players to stay in constant motion, creating more excitement.

- *Throw-In Violation* — a player must release the ball within 5 seconds of when an official gives it to him to start a throw-in. He cannot carry the ball inbounds, hand it to a teammate, bounce it out of bounds, or step on any part of a boundary line before he releases it.

- *Traveling* (*Walking* or Too Many Steps) — Traveling occurs when the ball handler takes more than one step without dribbling or releasing the basketball for a pass or shot. A player who is standing still when he receives a pass must keep his *pivot foot* on the floor until he is ready to dribble, shoot or pass the ball, whereas, a player who is moving when the ball comes to him can take a maximum of 2 steps in coming to a stop, passing or shooting. If a player falls with the ball he cannot slide. Also, a player may not catch his own missed shot before it touches the backboard, rim or another player. Traveling is one of the most overlooked violations in the *NBA*, as officials avoid interrupting the flow of the game for minor infractions.

- *Twenty-Four Second Violation* — the offense must attempt a field goal within 24 seconds of gaining possession of the ball (35 seconds for college men, 30 for college women and WNBA). If the ball has left a shooter's hands when the shot clock expires and it touches the rim of the basket, there is no violation and play can continue without a throw-in; if the ball goes into the basket, the field goal counts.

- *Other violations*
  - The ball cannot enter the basket from below or it will go to the team defending the basket.
  - A player cannot step out of bounds on his way to setting up a *screen*.

One type of violation is unique in that points are scored without the ball even going through the basket:

- *Goaltending* — if a defensive player touches a ball that is in the basket, partially in the area above the basket (the *cylinder*), or on its way down in its trajectory toward the basket (See **Fig. 20**), a 2-point field goal is automatically awarded to the offense. Touching the ball by putting a hand up through the basket ring or trapping the ball against the backboard are also goaltending. Generally, officials only call this if there was a chance for the ball to go into the basket without the interference. Only one point is awarded if the interference occurs during a free-throw attempt; 3 points if it occurs during a 3-point try.

Fig. 20: Goaltending or basket interference.

- *Basket Interference* — similar to goaltending except it is committed by an offensive player at his own basket and points are not automatically awarded. Instead, any basket scored is <u>not</u> counted and the opponents take possession for a throw-in. An offensive player is not called for interference for touching the ball in the cylinder if he is holding on to it for a shot, such as a *dunk*.

PERSONAL AND TEAM FOULS

Personal fouls can be called against an offensive or defensive player at any time during the game, including when the ball is dead. These fouls impose penalties for breaking the rules during the game. The league or *NCAA* may also impose additional fines or suspensions after a game. In general, a player on the court cannot push, hold, trip, elbow, restrain, hack or charge into his opponents. One important exception is that contact with the hand of an offensive player while it is touching the ball is not illegal because his hand is considered part of the ball. Most officials also overlook *incidental contact* and allow a minimal amount of hand-to-body contact by the defender (*handchecking*) as long as it does not affect a player's speed, quickness, balance or rhythm.

Keeping Track of Personal and Team Fouls

Each personal foul committed by a player is counted toward that player's total foul tally and his team's total foul tally. For example, the announcer will say "*Kobe Bryant* has just committed his 3rd personal foul. It is the Lakers' 6th team foul."

Since it is inevitable that contact will occur between players in the heat of battle and since players also commit fouls for strategic reasons (such as to prevent opponents from *freezing* the ball near the end of the game), a player is not disqualified from continuing to play in a game until he has committed 6 personal fouls (5 in college). It is common for a coach to insert a temporary substitute for a key player in *foul trouble* (usually one who has 4 or more fouls, or who has picked up 2 or 3 fouls early in the game). Once a player *fouls out*, a *substitute* must take his place for the rest of the game.

Over the Limit in Team Fouls

When an NBA team commits 5 or more team fouls per *period* (4 or more fouls in each *overtime*) that team is *over the limit* or *in the penalty* (8 per half for WNBA). For the remainder of the period, any non-shooting foul committed by that team (including the one that put it over the limit) will send the opponents to the free-throw line for 2 attempts instead of just awarding it with a throw-in. A team is also in the penalty as soon as it commits two fouls in the last 2 minutes of any period (including overtime), even if it has not yet reached a total of 5 for the entire period. In college, when a team has committed 7 or more fouls in any half, the opposing team goes to the line for a *1-and-1 opportunity* (if the first free-throw is missed, there is no second throw). After a team commits 10 fouls in a half, the opponents get to shoot 2 free throws regardless of whether they make the first one or not.

Types of Personal Fouls

A player cannot be guilty of a personal foul if he maintains his verticality. This means that he "owns" the space directly above him but he cannot lean into or reach over an opponent. There are several categories of behavior players cannot engage in, the most common of which are described here in alphabetical order:

- *Blocking, Illegal* — when a defensive player has <u>not</u> *established his position* (does not have both his feet firmly planted on the floor before the offensive player's head and shoulder get past him) and interferes with a ball handler's straight line movement. Defenders may also not use a hip movement that delays or prevents an opponent from moving. Blocking is the reverse of *charging*. (See **Fig. 21**)

Fig. 21: Charging or blocking foul.

- Charging — this is an *offensive foul* where a ball handler runs into a defender who has legally *established his position* (has both his feet firmly planted) instead of going around him or stopping. The defender must establish position before the offensive player's head and shoulder get past him. If the defender is moving when contact is made, he is called for illegal blocking, so defenders try to quickly get into position to "draw the charge" against the ball handler. Frequently, an official's judgment is all that separates a charge from an illegal blocking call.

- *Elbow Foul* — an elbow thrown by one player that makes contact with an opponent. That player is automatically ejected if the contact is made above the shoulder level, or even if below the shoulder level at the officials' discretion. An elbow thrown without contact is also a violation and can be assessed a technical foul.

- *Fighting* — particularly discouraged in college where ejections and suspensions from future games result from the first such act; suspension for the entire season including tournament play is the penalty for a second offense. In the pros, players are ejected, suspended and monetary fines levied.

- *Flagrant Foul* — when any foul committed is of such an unnecessary or excessive nature that injury could have resulted, such as punching and fighting. If the behavior is deemed unsporting, a player must be ejected. Its penalty is even harsher than a normal foul — not only does the wronged team get to shoot free-throw(s), but it also gets possession on a throw-in after the free-throw(s).

- Illegal Contact – a defensive player may not use his hand, forearm or body to make contact with the ball handler. However, there are several complicated exceptions to this rule (depending on the position of the ball handler in relation to the basket). To improve the flow of the game the NBA relaxed the incidental contact rule, and now officials ignore *handchecking* that does not affect a player's speed, quickness, balance or rhythm.

- *Loose Ball Foul* — illegal contact that occurs while neither team is in possession of a *live* ball.

- Offensive Foul (called a *Player-Control Foul* in college) — when a foul is committed by the ball handler, no free-throws are awarded but the foul is still counted toward the player's personal and team fouls tally.

- *Punching* — even if no contact is made, this leads to the automatic ejection of the player or non-player who threw it.

- *Pushing* or *Holding* — a foul by a defensive player for pushing the ball handler from the rear or by an offensive player guilty of pushing away a defender in his approach to the basket for a shot. Grabbing a player's uniform to interfere with his movement or pushing an opponent in the quest for a rebound are also illegal.

- *Screen, Illegal* — when an offensive player sets up a *screen* and is moving into his legal position, he must give the defensive player enough time to change direction and avoid a collision. An offensive player cannot sneak up behind an unsuspecting defender or take any position so close to a moving opponent that contact is inevitable (about 1 or 2 strides is adequate depending on the moving player's speed).

TECHNICAL FOULS

Technical fouls (also referred to as "Ts") are called for behavior officials feel violate fair play. Players can be cited for any unsporting conduct, breach of etiquette or dirty play (such as taunting or "trash talking", using obscenities or fouling an opponent after a ball is clearly whistled dead), and fighting (where participants are also subject to immediate ejection). Any disrespect toward officials, even without vulgarity (such as throwing a ball at them), can result in a technical, and players are never permitted to touch an official. Even tirades and continuous griping are not tolerated. Any excessive misconduct can lead to a player's ejection.

A technical foul awards a free-throw opportunity to the non-offending team. In the NBA and WNBA, 1 free-throw is awarded for every technical and the ball is then given to the team that had possession at the time the foul was called. In the case of *double technicals* simultaneously called on 2 players from opposing teams, no free-throws are taken. In college games the consequences of a technical are more serious, as 2 shots are awarded and the ball is given at midcourt to the non-offending team. For double technicals, both teams take two shots and the ball is given to the team the *possession arrow* designates.

When the technical is assessed, any player on the floor may take the free-throw, so teams generally choose their best free-throw shooter. Since the ball is awarded to a particular team after a technical free-throw, there is no need for either team to try to *rebound* a missed shot, so players do not line up along the foul lane as in a typical free-throw. In fact, in college they must all stand in the area beyond the *3-point line* and behind the *free-throw line extended*.

Misconduct by any non-players, such as coaches, is automatically called for a technical, as are some procedural fouls such as changing the *starting lineup* once submitted, having too many players on the court, calling too many timeouts or for the second offense of *delaying the game*. Coaches and their personnel can also be called for a "T" if they step outside the boundary lines of the *coaches' box*. They can leave this area only with an official's permission to help break up a fight (*coaches* only) or to talk with the *scorer* or *timer* during a dead ball.

It is not unusual for a coach to get a technical; sometimes this is a tactic intentionally used by the coach to motivate his players. However, when 2 technicals (3 in college) are called against a coach, he is ejected from the remainder of the game and must remain in his team's dressing room or leave the building. In college, any technicals called against anyone on the team are also counted against the head coach personally who is ejected after the third one.

AWAY FROM THE PLAY
An away-from-the-play foul is a foul committed by a defender before the offense releases a throw-in or on any

player without the ball (away from the play) in the final 2 minutes (final 1 minute in WNBA) of the fourth period or in overtime. The fouled team is awarded one free-throw (2 if it is an elbow or flagrant personal foul) which can be taken by any player in the game at the time of the foul, and it also takes the ball out of bounds for a throw-in.

DOUBLE FOULS

Double fouls, where 2 opponents commit personal or technical fouls against each other at the same time, cancel each other out and no free-throws are taken. While they are counted toward a player's foul total, they are not added to the team fouls. The next step depends on what was happening when the fouls were called:

- if one team was in possession of the ball when the double foul was called, it takes the ball out of bounds for a throw-in and the 24-second clock is reset
- if neither team was in possession or if the fouls occurred while the ball was in mid-air on an unsuccessful field goal attempt, then a jump ball between any 2 opponents on the floor is used to restart play
- if a field goal attempt was successful, the team scored against takes the throw-in to continue the game
- if the double foul is the result of a difference in opinion by the officials, a jump ball at the center circle resumes the action

Let us now take a look at **WOMEN'S BASKETBALL**.

WOMEN'S BASKETBALL

In the late 1990s professional women's basketball caught the public's attention across the U.S. Not one, but two leagues formed with the goal of bringing exciting, affordable basketball to a number of American cities and averaged as many as 9,000 fans a game. With basketball now the number one youth participation sport in the country for girls and with the additional exposure of television, women's basketball is likely to flourish. Many professional women players are former Olympians (including members of the 1996 and 2000 U.S. gold-medal teams), College Players of the Year (Naismith Award) or *NCAA Final Four MVPs*. Some have also played in professional leagues overseas.

AMERICAN BASKETBALL LEAGUE

The *American Basketball League (ABL)* was formed in 1996 with 9 teams divided into 2 *conferences*. Initially it attracted talent by paying more than the rival *Women's National Basketball Association (WNBA)*, but in 1998 it went bankrupt and was merged into the WNBA.

WOMEN'S NATIONAL BASKETBALL ASSOCIATION

The WNBA was launched in 1997 and plays during the summer months (June-August) to garner the greatest television exposure during a quiet period in professional team sports. Through their affiliation with the *NBA*, WNBA athletes have participated in the NBA's *All-Star* Saturday since 1998. In 1999 a separate WNBA All-Star game was added in mid-season.

The league began with 8 teams divided into two conferences, and quickly expanded to 10 in 1998, then to 16 by 2002 after the merger with the ABL.

Eastern Conference	Western Conference
Charlotte Sting[+]	Houston Comets[**+]
Cleveland Rockers[+]	Los Angeles Sparks[+]
Detroit Shock[*]	Minnesota Lynx
Indiana Fever	Phoenix Mercury[+]
Miami Sol	Portland Fire
New York Liberty[+]	Sacramento Monarchs[+]
Orlando Miracle	Seattle Storm
Washington Mystics[*]	Utah Starzz[+]

[+] original 8
[*]1998 addition
[**]began in the Eastern Conference

In order to qualify to play for the WNBA, a player must be at least 22 years old, and either have completed collegiate basketball eligibility or played at least 2 years of professional basketball with another league. It is not surprising that the average WNBA player is a mature 25.8 years old with four years of professional playing experience. The women also average $5'11\frac{3}{4}''$ in height and 167.9 pounds in weight.

The WNBA elected to develop its own set of rules, borrowing elements from the NBA and women's NCAA rules. **Table 2** highlights some of the more important similarities and differences between the various leagues.

TABLE 2: RULE COMPARISONS

Rule	NCAA*	NBA	WNBA
3-point line	19'9"	23'9" arc/22' on sides	19'9"
Court length	94' x 50'	94' x 50'	94' x 50'
Lane size	12' wide	16' wide	12' wide
Ball size	maximum 30 inches	about 30 inches	maximum 29 inches
Active Roster	10	12	10
Game Duration	two 20-min. halves	four 12-min. quarters	two 20-min. halves
Halftime	15 minutes	15 minutes	15 minutes
Overtime	5 minutes	5 minutes	5 minutes
Shot Clock	35 seconds (30 for women)	24 seconds	30 seconds
Shot Clock Reset	FG attempt hits rim	FG attempt hits rim	FG attempt hits rim
Jump Ball	At start of game, then possession alternates	Start of each half; for certain violations	Start of each half; for certain violations
Player Foul Limit	5	6	6
Flagrant, Intentional and Technical Foul Penalties	Technical, Flagrant and Intentional Fouls all result in 2 FT + ball	Flagrant or Intentional 2 FT + ball; Technical 1 FT	Flagrant or Intentional 2 FT + ball; Technical 1 FT
Team Fouls/Bonus FT	After 7 team fouls per half shoots 1+1; 10 team fouls shoots 2	After 5 team fouls per period (4 in OT) or after 2 team fouls in last 2 minutes of any period (including OT), shoots 2	After 8 team fouls per half (3 in OT) or after 2 team fouls in last minute of any period (including OT), shoots 2
Free-Throw Positions	2 bottom lane spaces must be occupied	4 bottom lane spaces must be occupied	4 bottom lane spaces must be occupied
Time-Outs called by	Coach or player	Player	Player
Advancing Ball after a Time-Out	This option not available	After full TO in last 2 minutes of game or OT, can select midcourt or designated out-of-bounds spot.	After full or :20 TO in last minute of game or OT, can select midcourt or designated out-of-bounds spot.
Time-Outs – not TV	4 full (75 seconds) and two 30 seconds per game	6 full (100 seconds if mandatory or 60 seconds if not) and two 20 seconds per game	1 full (120 seconds) and one 20 seconds each half; plus 1 added 20 seconds in 2nd half
Time-Outs – TV	1 full (60 seconds) and 4 30 seconds per game plus TV commercial time-outs	Same as not TV	Same as not TV
Time-Outs – Overtime	All unused full and 30 seconds carry over; plus 1 additional full	Three new full 60-second TOs; no carry overs	Maximum of 1 unused 20 seconds from 2nd half carries over; plus 1 additional full and one 20 seconds
5-seconds violation	Yes	No	No
Number of officials	2 or 3	3	3
Game Clock Stops After Successful FG	In last minute of regulation or OT. No subs allowed.	Last minute of quarters 1-3; last 2 minutes of regulation or OT	Last minute of each half and OT
Selection of Player to Replace Injured for FTs	Coach of same team selects	Coach of opposing team selects	Coach of opposing team selects
8 or 10-second rule	10 seconds (women NA)	8 seconds	10 seconds
Legal Jersey Numbers	00, 0, 1-5, 10-15, 20-25, 30-35, 40-45, 50-55	00, 0, 3-55	00, 0, 3-55

* With few exceptions, the NCAA College Rules for men and women are the same.

THINGS TO LOOK FOR DURING PLAY / STRATEGY

To those spectators who simply watch the ball in a basketball game, it may seem that successful *field goals* are just a matter of good luck, and *fouls* called against a team just a matter of bad luck. In truth, scoring is achieved through a series of well-orchestrated moves between teammates in the face of close scrutiny by defenders who try to stop them. And although fouls are usually committed by accident, they are often the result of good deceptive moves on the part of the fouled player. Learning how to spot these plays takes practice, but it can greatly increase your enjoyment in watching the game.

MATCH-UPS

A *match-up* is defined as any pairing of players on opposing teams who *guard* each other during a game. These pairings are vital as coaches try to exploit each opponent's known weaknesses when there are *mismatches* (a smaller or slower player against a bigger or faster one). Coaches try to avoid being on the short end of a mismatch, assigning players to guard opponents with similar abilities. As one team makes *substitutions*, the other needs to adjust its match-ups.

WHERE TO LOOK

First rid yourself of bad habits: do not just concentrate on the ball. Instead, try to absorb all 10 players on the court and allow yourself to find patterns. Keep in mind the court is divided into 3 invisible "lanes" — the middle area where the *key* is and 2 "wing lanes" along the sides of the court. The offense generally looks to move toward the "open lane" (the one with the least number of players). This forces the defense to spread out, making its job more difficult.

Look for the number of players moving on the court. If there are 1 or 2 players in the *post* standing still, they will become the hub of the activity as their teammates move around them. Remember to watch the *ball handler* (not just the ball) even <u>after</u> he has passed the ball to figure out if he is setting himself up to get it back again.

HALF-COURT OFFENSE

The opposite of the fast break is the *half-court offense* or *set offense* where a team takes the time to develop a play in its *frontcourt*. The next few sections give examples of plays a team tries in this type of offense.

The Give-and-Go

One of the most basic plays on offense, the *give-and-go*, occurs when one player (a giver or passer) passes the ball to a teammate (a *receiver*), "cuts" to the basket and then gets the ball back as soon as he is *open*. What makes this sequence successful is that the defender who was guarding the giver relaxes slightly when the ball is passed to another player. As soon as he slackens his defense, the giver is able to get open to get the ball back and *drive* to the basket or shoot.

Screening Plays

A *screening play* is any play where one offensive player (the *screener*) gives his teammate room by standing between him and a defender. (See **Fig. 22**) This *screen* (or *pick*) often gives the teammate a chance to take an open shot with no defender in his face. The most effective screens are set by big players such as *forwards* and *centers* to free up their smaller teammates from defenders. While watching play, any time you see an offensive player just standing in the middle of the frontcourt with his hands to his sides not even looking for the ball, he is probably looking to set up a screen. There are several types of screening plays you should learn to recognize:

Pinch-Post — similar to the give-and-go, except the giver passes to an open teammate in the post who acts as the screener. The giver then *fakes* to one side but cuts to the other side close to the screener, preventing his defender

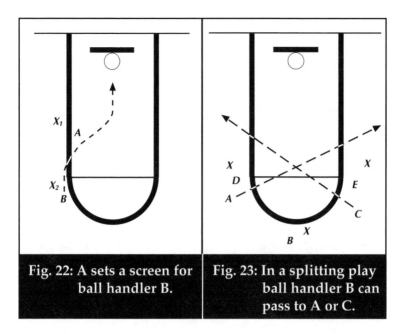

| Fig. 22: A sets a screen for ball handler B. | Fig. 23: In a splitting play ball handler B can pass to A or C. |

from staying with him. This defender has been "picked off" by the screener, leaving the giver open to get the ball back from the screener and shoot it.

Backdoor — this is a 3-player variation of the give-and-go where a player who was not the original giver is the one who gets open and is given the ball to shoot instead. When the defenders all concentrate on the pass to the *post* they often ignore a player behind them on the wing who is open to then receive the pass from the post, and go in for a *layup*.

Pick-and-roll or *Screen-and-roll* — after screening an opponent to get a teammate free, the screener rolls (or pivots) toward the basket to receive a pass from the ball handler and shoot. The shot will usually be a layup.

SPLITTING
Splitting is a 3-person play where 2 players (called *cutters*) crisscross as they cut past the post to give a ball handler the option of passing the ball to either one. (See **Fig. 23**)

These splitting plays are usually aided by screens:

Double Screen — this splitting pattern has the passer and one of the cutters stop at the post to provide a *double screen* for the other cutter. These are particularly helpful to *perimeter* shooters or if one of the screeners is able to get free and roll to the basket.

Stack — 2 big teammates standing in the *low post* on the same side of the *foul lane* set screens for each other or a double screen for a teammate. Usually this pattern uses a screen by the center to get a forward free.

ONE-ON-ONE PLAYS

Sometimes 4 offensive players will clear a path for a *one-on-one* showdown between their most talented player and a defender (also called a *clear out*). These 4 teammates set up a stack on both sides of the middle lane while the one-on-one moves to the top of the key. In this position they are available to receive a pass if the defense *double teams* their ball handler.

AWAY FROM THE PLAY

After you identify one of the basic offensive plays in basketball described above, look to see what the other players are doing — what is going on away from the ball will tell more of the story. These other players may be

- standing still and observing
- moving into defensive position for a transition
- preparing for an alternative offensive play
- positioning themselves for a rebound
- positioning themselves for a pass

It is important to pay attention to how well a team sets screens on the *weakside* (the side away from the ball) and how the defense is responding, because this is often where the next play develops. In a game as rapid as basketball, the spectator needs to stay a few steps ahead — you can follow the action better if you identify several possible upcoming plays.

FAST BREAK

The *fast break* (or the *run and shoot*) is one of the most exciting plays to watch and one of the easiest ways for a smaller, quicker team to score. Generally, this play begins when a player grabs a missed shot at one end (*defensive rebound*) and immediately sends an *outlet pass* toward *midcourt* where most of his teammates are waiting. These teammates can sprint to reach their basket and quickly shoot before enough of their opponents catch up to stop them. By outnumbering the defense, this pattern provides an easy opportunity to score or to get *offensive rebounds* in case the shot is missed.

Here are some patterns you might see, where the first digit of the notation represents the number of players on offense during the fast break and the second digit represents the number of players on defense:

3-on-2 break — the most common variety, where 2 offensive players run down the two wing lanes a few feet ahead of the ball handler who runs down the middle lane. (In addition, a few feet behind and to one side of the ball handler is the trailer who is ready to take a *jump shot* off a *blind pass*. The fifth offensive player is the rebounder who initiated the fast break who waits back in defensive position prepared for a quick *transition*.) Since there are only 2 defenders, one of the 3 offensive players will remain open when the defenders commit themselves to guarding 2 of them, and the ball handler needs to make a quick decision — to pass to an open teammate or take the ball to the basket himself.

2-on-1 break — the goal of the offense here is to make the lone defender commit to guarding one player so the ball handler can decide to go in himself for a layup or pass to his teammate. The longer a defender waits to commit, the more he forces the ball handler to go all the way to the basket himself.

3-on-1 break — this provides a huge advantage for the offense because 2 of its players are unguarded and can pass freely among themselves, almost always resulting in a score. However, the defender's teammates are ready to greatly outnumber the opponent for any play at the other end.

FULL COURT PRESS

When several defenders start to pressure the offense in the *backcourt*, it is called a *full-court press*. The press can disrupt some teams by hindering them from bringing the ball into the frontcourt and causing *turnovers* near the opponent's basket.

Fig. 24: Double team.

TYPES OF DEFENSES
Man-to-Man Defense
In the *man-to-man defense* each player on the defending team is responsible for guarding a particular player on the opposing team. In this type of defense, a defender sometimes "picks up" his player as soon as the ball is brought *inbounds* in the backcourt in an attempt to cause an *8-second violation* or turnover closer to the defender's own basket. When 2 defenders join forces to guard against a single offensive player, it is called a *double team* (See **Fig. 24**).

Zone Defense
In a *zone defense*, each defender is responsible for an area of the court, and he must guard any player who ventures into that area. Usually, as soon as the ball enters a zone, the defender of that area will get some assistance from one or more of his teammates. The zone defense is used extensively at the college level, but was outlawed in the NBA from 1961 to 2001 (where it was called *illegal defense*) as the league tried to promote more exciting one-on-one match-ups. Starting with the 2001-02 season, the zone defense was allowed again in the NBA, but its return has not changed the game very much for two key reasons: 1) an extra defender in one part of the floor leaves a player open elsewhere, and defenders are wary of leaving open very accurate NBA shooters, and 2) the league added an unprecedented 3-second rule for defenders; to stay *in the paint* for more than 3 seconds, a defender must be guarding a player there, so players cannot play zone near the basket.

There are 3 general types of zone defenses: the 3-2, the 2-3 and the 1-3-1. (See **Fig. 25**) The numbers describe the position of the defenders as seen by the offense from midcourt. Which defense a team employs will depend on the relative strengths and weaknesses of its players and those of its opponents:

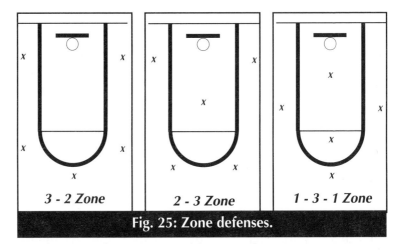

Fig. 25: Zone defenses.

3-2 zone — 3 defenders are positioned across the court in front of the *foul circle* with 2 on the outer sides of the *foul lane.* Considered an offensive zone, it prepares a team to make a quick transition to a fast break with more players close to their basket.

2-3 zone — this is more of a defensive zone that sets up 3 players near the basket to prevent the offense from getting a close shot or a layup. This is the defense preferred by teams with taller, slower players who are less likely to fast break.

1-3-1 zone— also a defensive zone which sets up 1 player outside each side of the foul lane and 3 players in a line from the foul line to below the basket who will fall back to form a tight triangle below the basket as the offense advances. This is the defense sometimes used when the offensive team has at least one player who is good at shooting or passing from the top of the key because it places a defender there while the 3-2 and 2-3 defenses do not.

Man-to-Man vs. Zone

The man-to-man defense gives offensive players less room to shoot from the *outside* (or *perimeter*) than the zone because each player is guarded by a defender specifically assigned to him, whereas zone defenders merely cover an area. However, zone defenses are better able to stop a dominant offensive player from scoring *inside* because defenders provide help to overmatched teammates in nearby zones.

THREE-POINT SHOOTING

Three-point shots ignite the fans and boost a team's morale. They can change a game very quickly—even a 9 point deficit can be erased by just 3 baskets when a team has good 3-point shooters. Teams like to put their best shooters on the floor whenever they are way behind with time running out, so look for substitutions to insert these shooters and watch them try to get open for 3-point opportunities. A team with great 3-point shooters does more than just score points in big chunks, though. It also forces the defense to guard them more closely away from the basket, drawing defenders away from its inside players to make it easier for them to score.

TIMEOUTS

While they are precious and usually saved for the most critical moments, *timeouts* can be used by a team in a number of strategic ways:

- to stop its opponent's momentum when it is on a *run*
- since a timeout in the last 2 minutes of an NBA game allows the offense to inbound the ball at midcourt instead of way back in the backcourt, a team uses it when it needs to save precious seconds and avoid the potential for an *8-second violation*
- in the final minutes of a close game, a team ready for a *throw-in* may use up a timeout just to change its play in response to how it observed the defense setting up for the throw-in and upcoming play
- if the defense is particularly tight on any throw-in and the thrower is unable to get the ball inbounds within the allotted 5 seconds, he may call a timeout rather than commit the violation and lose *possession*

- at any point during play that a player feels he is about to commit a turnover, he may call for a timeout and receive a temporary reprieve as his team meets to talk things over on the *sidelines*

END OF PERIOD STRATEGIES
Playing the Clock
Teams who are leading near the end of a game can employ a series of time-related strategies to slow the pace down. The logic is that the longer a team holds the ball, the fewer opportunities its opponents will have to catch up. In playing the clock, a team waits until most of the *shot clock* has expired before shooting and then takes only high percentage shots. To pass the time, it moves slowly with the ball, dribbling or passing frequently around the perimeter. Near the end of a close game, these delay tactics inspire opponents to purposely commit fouls since the clock stops during free-throws and they get possession after the attempts.

Intentional Fouling and Free-Throws
When intentionally fouling an opponent to stop the clock, a team clearly wants to foul the player with the least likelihood of completing his free-throw attempt — one with a low *free-throw percentage* (65% or less). However, the defense must be careful not to commit a *flagrant foul*, which would also give the fouled team possession after the free-throws. The team that knows it is going to get fouled tries to keep the ball in the hands of its player with the best free-throw percentage (80% or higher). Since time is running out, the defense usually cannot wait until the ball is in the right player's hands to commit the foul, giving the offense the advantage.

Now that you are on your way to identifying plays and strategies, it is time to introduce you to the structure of professional basketball in the U.S. Let us examine the **NBA TEAMS, DIVISIONS & CONFERENCES**.

NBA TEAMS, DIVISIONS & CONFERENCES

As of the 2002-03 season, the *National Basketball Association* (*NBA*) had 29 teams divided into 4 *divisions* and 2 *conferences*. The names of these divisions and conferences generally reflect the geographic regions represented by the teams.

Eastern Conference:
- *Atlantic Division* (7 teams)
- *Central Division* (8 teams)

Western Conference:
- *Pacific Division* (7 teams)
- *Midwest Division* (7 teams)

An example of how the actual NBA teams are listed in the newspaper is located in the chapter **DECIPHERING STATISTICS IN THE NEWSPAPER**.

THE BIRTH OF THE NBA

The precursors to the NBA were the *National Basketball League* (*NBL*) and the *Basketball Association of America* (*BAA*). All 3 leagues changed their size many times over the years through *expansion* that came from the creation of new teams, the addition of existing teams from outside the league and by mergers with other leagues.

The NBL was formed in 1937, and though its progress was sidetracked by World War II, it continued to add *franchises* through the late 1940s. The BAA was started at the end of the war by operators of large National Hockey League arenas who wanted to make greater use of their facilities and capitalize on the growing popularity of basketball. Only 3 of the original 11 teams that began the BAA's first season in 1946 remain in the NBA today — the *Boston Celtics*, New York Knickerbockers and Philadelphia Warriors (who later moved to San Francisco).

Though the Baltimore Bullets joined the BAA in 1947-48, it was not until 1948-49 that the league experienced its first official expansion when the 4 best teams of the rival NBL (Fort Wayne Pistons, Indianapolis Jets, Minneapolis Lakers and Rochester Royals) joined the BAA's Western Division.

The NBA finally came into existence as the last 6 NBL teams were absorbed into the BAA in 1949-50, and the entire league with its 17 teams and 3 divisions was renamed. Its teams were:

Eastern Division:	Central Division:	Western Division:
Baltimore Bullets*	Chicago Stags	Anderson Packers
Boston Celtics*	Fort Wayne Pistons*	Denver Nuggets
NY Knickerbockers*	Minneapolis Lakers*	Indianapolis Olympians*
Philadelphia Warriors*	Rochester Royals*	Sheboygen (Wis) Redskins
Syracuse Nationals*	St. Louis Bombers	Tri-Cities Blackhawks*
Washington Capitols*		Waterloo (Iowa) Hawks

By the 1950-51 season only 11 teams remained (* above) and in subsequent seasons the league stabilized at 8 teams. The league did not grow again until 10 years later when the Chicago Packers (who later became the Baltimore/ Washington Bullets) joined in 1961, followed by the Chicago Bulls in 1966. Two more franchises were added the next year (Seattle Supersonics and San Diego/Houston Rockets), and 2 more the year after that (Phoenix Suns and Milwaukee Bucks).

THE ABA MERGER

Meanwhile, the *American Basketball Association (ABA)* came into existence in 1967 with 11 teams, and added 2 more in 1968. Financial woes plagued the new league so it was not long before the ABA began contemplating a merger with the NBA. By 1970, the NBA had expanded to 17 teams and split into the 4 divisions and 2 conferences which remain in existence today. The NBA's 18th team, the New Orleans Jazz, joined the Central Division in 1974.

The merger with the ABA finally took place in 1976, adding the Denver Nuggets, Indiana Pacers, New York (later New Jersey) Nets and San Antonio Spurs, requiring a major realignment of the then-22 NBA teams into different divisions. A few more relocations (Los Angeles Clippers, Sacramento Kings and Utah Jazz) and one expansion (Dallas Mavericks in 1980) marked the early 1980s.

RECENT EXPANSION
The late 1980s brought aggressive expansion by the NBA as it introduced 4 new teams in 2 years:

Charlotte Hornets (1988)   Miami Heat (1988)
Minnesota Timberwolves (1989)   Orlando Magic (1989)

In 1995, the NBA's expansion efforts moved outside the United States for the first time, as 2 Canadian teams were added (one of which later moved to the U.S.):

Toronto Raptors (1995)   Vancouver Grizzlies (1995)

LIST OF CURRENT NBA TEAMS
Table 3 is an alphabetized list of each NBA team, the year it joined the league, and its division and conference:

Table 3: Current NBA Teams

Team	Year	Division	Conference
Atlanta Hawks[1]	1949	Central	Eastern
Boston Celtics	1946	Atlantic	Eastern
Chicago Bulls	1966	Central	Eastern
Cleveland Cavaliers	1970	Central	Eastern
Dallas Mavericks	1980	Midwest	Western
Denver Nuggets	1976	Midwest	Western
Detroit Pistons[2]	1948	Central	Eastern
Golden State Warriors[3]	1946	Pacific	Western
Houston Rockets[4]	1967	Midwest	Western
Indiana Pacers	1976	Central	Eastern
Los Angeles Clippers[5]	1970	Pacific	Western
Los Angeles Lakers[6]	1948	Pacific	Western
Memphis Grizzlies[7]	1995	Midwest	Western
Miami Heat	1988	Atlantic	Eastern
Milwaukee Bucks	1968	Central	Eastern
Minnesota Timberwolves	1989	Midwest	Western
New Jersey Nets[8]	1976	Atlantic	Eastern
New Orleans Hornets[9]	1988	Central	Eastern
New York Knickerbockers[10]	1946	Atlantic	Eastern
Orlando Magic	1989	Atlantic	Eastern
Philadelphia 76ers[11]	1949	Atlantic	Eastern
Phoenix Suns	1968	Pacific	Western
Portland Trailblazers	1970	Pacific	Western
Sacramento Kings[12]	1948	Pacific	Western
San Antonio Spurs	1976	Midwest	Western
Seattle Sonics[13]	1967	Pacific	Western
Toronto Raptors	1995	Central	Eastern
Utah Jazz[14]	1974	Midwest	Western
Washington Wizards[15]	1961	Atlantic	Eastern

[1] Tri-Cities Blackhawks '49-'51; Milwaukee Hawks '51-'55, St. Louis Hawks '55-'68
[2] Fort Wayne Pistons '48-'57
[3] Philadelphia Warriors '46-'62; San Francisco Warriors '62-'71
[4] San Diego Rockets '67-'71
[5] Buffalo Braves '70-'78; San Diego Clippers '78-'84
[6] Minneapolis Lakers '48-'60
[7] Vancouver Grizzlies '95-'01
[8] New York Nets '76-'77
[9] Charlotte Hornets '88-'02
[10] More commonly called the New York Knicks
[11] Syracuse Nationals '49-'63
[12] Rochester Royals '48-'57; Cincinnati Royals '57-'72; Kansas City-Omaha Kings '72-'75; Kansas City Kings '75-'85
[13] Seattle Supersonics '67-'94
[14] New Orleans Jazz '74-'80
[15] Chicago Packers '61-'62; Chicago Zephyrs '62-'63; Baltimore Bullets '63-'73, Capital Bullets '73-'74; Washington Bullets '75-'97

NBA SEASON & PLAYOFFS

REGULAR SEASON

The *NBA* begins its 82-game *regular season* the first Friday in November, ending the 3rd Sunday in April. Since a season overlaps 2 calendar years, it is referred to by both (e.g., the 2003-04 season). A team usually plays half of its games at home and half on the road. Teams within a single *conference* will meet most often, playing against each other a minimum of 3-4 times during the season and creating intense regional rivalries. NBA teams also play every team in the league (including teams in the other conference) twice — once at home and once on the road — to promote national rivalries as well. Since 1990, a few of these games have been played abroad each season.

During regular-season play, the 29 NBA teams compete for the top spots in the *standings*. Teams are ranked within each *division* based on a simple *win-loss* or *winning percentage* (no game ever ends in a *tie* in the NBA). The team with the best *record* (the highest winning percentage) is the *division leader*. More on standings is discussed in the chapter on **DECIPHERING STATISTICS IN THE NEWSPAPER**.

PLAYOFFS

After the regular-season schedule of games is over, the 16 teams with the best overall records advance to the *post-season*, otherwise known as the NBA *playoffs*. The dates for the playoffs vary each year depending on how long each *round* lasts, but generally they begin in late April and last until mid-June. As the regular season draws to a close, teams "clinch" playoff spots as soon as their records assure they will be in the top 16.

The top 8 teams in each of the 2 conferences advance to the playoffs. There are 4 rounds played to narrow the number of teams by eliminating the losers of each. Teams are paired up to play a *best-of-seven series* in each of the rounds, which means the first team to win 4 games emerges victorious. This can be done in as few as 4, 5, or 6 games, although the more evenly matched 2 teams are, the more likely a series will go the full 7 games. Over a 7-game series it is less likely that a weaker team will get lucky and advance to the next round than if a single game was played. Before 2002-03, the first round of the playoffs had been decided by a *best-of-five series* that led to several remarkable *upsets*, prompting the change to a *best-of-seven*.

The 16 playoff teams are *seeded* #1 - #8 within each of the 2 conferences. The 8 teams within each conference play each other in 4 head-to-head series. Within each conference, the division leader with the best record is seeded #1. The other division leader is seeded number #2, even if this team's record is not the second best in the entire conference. The teams with the next 6 best records from either division are seeded #3 through #8. For this reason, one division may be represented by more teams than the other.

In the first round, the #1 team in each conference plays against the #8 in the conference, #2 vs. #7, #3 vs. #6, and #4 vs. #5. (See **Fig. 26**) The 4 winners within each conference play each other in the second round, also called the *conference semifinals*. Two teams advance to each *conference final* (or third round), where the winner is crowned conference champion.

These 2 conference champions meet in the fourth, or final round, called the *NBA Finals*, to determine the best team in the league. The winner is permanently awarded a *Larry O'Brien Trophy*. Although there can be a new champion every year, some teams have established dynasties, winning the trophy several years in succession. For more on this, see the chapter on **GREAT TEAMS & DYNASTIES**. Each player and important member of a championship team also receives a large jeweled *ring* to keep.

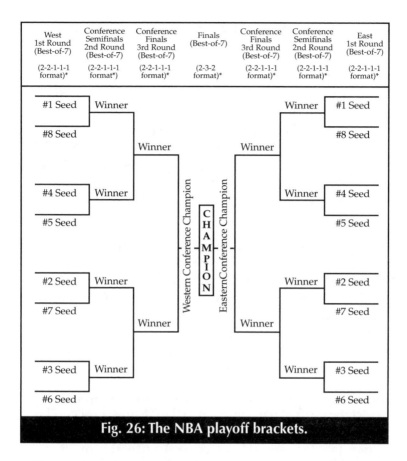

Fig. 26: The NBA playoff brackets.

* The number of games played at one site before changing sites; each series begins with 2 home games for the team seeded higher.

NBA ALL-STAR GAME & TEAMS

ALL-STAR GAME

The idea of holding a mid-season game featuring the best players from different *NBA* teams was born in 1951. The first *All-Star Game* was nearly canceled though, as most people, including the league's *Commissioner Maurice Podoloff*, thought it would flop. It was only at the insistence of the indomitable Walter Brown (then-owner of the *Boston Celtics*) who took over responsibility for its expenses and potential losses, that the game was held.

Today, it is one of the most exciting events in sports. Beginning in 1984, it was expanded into an entire All-Star Weekend held mid-season (usually in February). The festivities include a Legends game, a series of contests from slam dunking to long distance shooting, and educational programming for kids the day before Sunday's All-Star Game. In 1998, the first event including *WNBA* players was added. The location is changed every year.

Fans submit ballots (found at games or in newspapers) to select the top 5 players on each of the 2 teams, East and West, representing the 2 *conferences*. The player(s) at each position (*guard(s)*, *forward(s)* and *center*) with the most votes automatically starts the game for his conference. Each All-Star team is led by the *coach* of the NBA team with the best *record* in that conference on the balloting deadline date, accompanied by the assistant coaches he regularly works with. It is the league's coaches who select 7 additional *reserves* per team to round out the *roster* and create a *bench*.

The All-Star Game is unique in that every player on each team will see some playing time — after all, it is a spectacle for the pleasure of the fans. Since the emphasis is on exciting offensive plays, the scores of these contests are much higher than those of most regular NBA games. A definite rivalry divides the nation, although through 2002, the East had won 33 games to the West's 18 victories (there was no game in 1999 due to a *lockout*).

NBA LOTTERY, DRAFT, TRADES, FREE AGENCY & LABOR ISSUES

THE NBA DRAFT & LOTTERY

The *NBA* teams select, or *draft*, new team members from among a pool of candidates, most of whom are recent college graduates or talented foreign players. Occasionally, talented and hopeful underclassmen test their chances by leaving school early — a scenario that has become more common with the passage in 1997 of an *NCAA* rule permitting such players to return to college if they are disappointed with how they fare in the draft (as long as they have not hired an agent). In 2002, another NCAA rule extended a similar privilege to high school athletes. A *lottery* to determine draft order is held during the *halftime* break of a *playoff* game — usually in late May — about 1 month before the actual draft takes place in late June.

One purpose of the draft is to maintain balanced competition throughout the league by affording those teams with the worst *win-loss records* the opportunity to obtain the best available talent first and thereby improve in subsequent years. Sometimes a team will select the best player at a position that team needs to fill on its *roster*. Each selection is made during a *round* (where each team gets a turn to make a pick). Although the NBA held its first college draft prior to the start of the 1947-48 season, the idea of using rounds was not introduced until 1957. In past years there have been as many as 21 rounds, but today there are only 2 rounds in each draft.

To assure that teams did not purposely lose ("throw") their final games to get a top *draft pick*, teams used a simple coin flip to determine the selection sequence up through 1984. Beginning in June 1985, the NBA Board of Governors adopted a lottery system for non-playoff teams to determine the order of selection in the first round of the NBA draft. In all succeeding rounds, teams picked in the inverse order of their win-loss records. The lottery was later modified to guarantee that the last team in the NBA would, in the worse case, receive the 4th pick in the draft.

The draft was altered yet again in 1990, for the then-11 non-playoff teams, to provide a weighted system that gave the team with the worst record the greatest chance of obtaining the number 1 pick (#11 had 11 numbered ping-pong balls in a drum, #10 had 10 balls, #2 had 2 balls, etc). This served the NBA well until 1993, when the Orlando Magic defied statistical probability and obtained the number 1 pick for the second consecutive year, despite having the best overall record among non-playoff teams (a 1 out of 66 — or 1.5% — chance of occurrence).

The "Orlando repeat incident" prompted the NBA to revamp its lottery yet again. The new system uses 14 balls numbered 1-14. The procedure involves drawing 4 balls to create one of 1,001 4-number combinations ($14 \times 13 \times 12 \times 11 / 4 \times 3 \times 2 \times 1$). The team with the worst record is assigned 250 of these 1,001 combinations for a 25% chance of obtaining the number 1 pick. The team with the second worst record gets 203 (or a 20.3% chance), etc. This new system also drastically reduces the likelihood of a team with the best record among non-playoff contenders (like Orlando in 1993) getting the number 1 pick from 1.5% to 0.5%.

EXPANSION & OTHER DRAFTS

Whenever the NBA adds teams through *expansion* (1966, 1968, 1970, 1974, 1980, 1988, 1989 and 1995), a separate *expansion draft* is held where each existing team is permitted to protect a number of its most important players, leaving the others available for selection by the expansion team(s). A number of other drafts have been held over the last 2 decades, including the 1971 Hardship Drafts (following a lawsuit requiring the NBA and *ABA* to include underclassmen in their drafts), the 1972 and 1976 ABA Dispersal Drafts (to absorb players from dissolved ABA teams into the NBA), and the 1973 ABA Special Circumstances Draft.

SALARY CAP & FREE AGENCY

Even though a player is drafted by a team, he must still negotiate a contract. The NBA has tried to prevent having players' salaries spiral out of control by establishing a *salary cap*, limiting the dollar amount a team can pay all of its players collectively in a season. Players can sign a variety of contracts up to several years in length but since 1995, 1st round picks must sign a minimum length contract (increased from 3 to 4 years in 1998). At the expiration of this contract, a player becomes a *free agent*. At that point, his team can re-negotiate with him, or another team can make an offer. However, if the player is a *restricted free agent*, his current team has the *right of first refusal*, allowing it to counter any other team's offer within 15 days. As long as the current team's counteroffer matches the key terms of the other team's deal, the player is obligated to stay with his current team. A team does not have this right of first refusal with an *unrestricted free agent*.

TRADES
Teams are allowed to trade players on their rosters, players who have been drafted and draft choices. These trades can include the rights to future draft picks as incentives. The NBA *trading deadline* (the 16th Thursday of the season which usually falls in February) is an important time to watch for a flurry of trading activity. After this date, no players can be traded for the remainder of that season.

LABOR NEGOTIATIONS
When the NBA's first *collective bargaining agreement* expired in 1994-95, heated negotiations led to the league's first *lockout* (July-September 1995), then to a renewed 6-year agreement. A second lockout lasted only 3 hours as details were finalized in July 1996. However, dissatisfied owners exercised their right to re-open negotiations only 3 years into this agreement, and on July 1, 1998 imposed a 3rd lockout. At issue was the division of *basketball-related income (BRI)* and the salary cap. The agreement dedicated 48% of BRI to player salaries, but in 1997 owners paid 57% of BRI largely due to the *"Larry Bird Exception"* which allowed teams to exceed the salary cap to sign their own free agents. This time negotiations failed, the first games in NBA history were cancelled, and by January 6, 1999 it was feared the entire season would be lost. However, a secret all-night session between *David Stern* and the players' union led to a new 6-year deal and an abbreviated season was saved.

THE NCAA & THE FINAL FOUR

THE NCAA

The *National Collegiate Athletic Association* (*NCAA*) is a voluntary association comprised of over 1,200 colleges, universities and related organizations in the U.S., from large state institutions to small, privately funded colleges. The role of the NCAA is to protect the integrity of amateurism for student-athletes, and assist these educational institutions in establishing standards and determining the proper role of athletics within their programs. A number of committees develop the NCAA's overall policies and procedures, and the specific rules for each of the 21 sports it administers.

The NCAA enforces the rules and regulations the colleges vote to impose upon themselves. In recent years the NCAA has taken an aggressive view toward violations of these rules and standards, and has meted out punishments that include monetary fines and suspension from tournament participation for several years. The NCAA has the power to limit the playing time of a particular athlete or can even prevent a school from televising its games, thereby affecting an individual's career potential or the college's recruiting ability in the future. It also imposes a variety of educational requirements designed to prepare athletes for the real world (since the average *NBA* career — for the few who make it — is only 3.5 years). Many colleges have clubs of alumni supporting certain sports who call themselves *boosters*, but they are unrelated to the NCAA.

COLLEGE TEAMS & CONFERENCES

In basketball, the colleges themselves are divided into 3 *divisions*, based on their competitive level: Divisions I, II and III, with I being the best. Only Divisions I and II offer athletic scholarships. The schools are further divided into *conferences*. Listed below are the various conferences (those marked with an * are better-known and usually represented by more than one team in the NCAA tournament each year):

America East	Conference USA	Pacific-10 (Pac 10)*
Atlantic Coast (ACC)*	Horizon League	Patriot League
Atlantic Sun	Ivy League	Southeastern*
Atlantic 10*	Metro Atlantic	(East & West)
Big East*	Mid-American	Southern
Big Sky	Mid-Continent	Southland
Big South	Mid-Eastern Athletic	Southwestern Athletic
Big Ten*	Missouri Valley	Sun Belt
Big 12*	Mountain West	West Coast
Big West	Northeast	Western Athletic
Colonial Athletic	Ohio Valley	

Each team plays a schedule of *regular-season* games from mid-November through March of the next year, mostly against the teams within the same conference (intraconference) and a handful against teams in other conferences (interconference). Only the intraconference games count toward determining each conference's champion. *Exhibition* games played prior to or during the season are not counted as part of a team's *record*.

THE NCAA TOURNAMENT & FINAL FOUR

The *NCAA Tournament* has been in existence since 1939 when only 8 teams competed. Expansion of the field took place over time: 16 teams in 1951, 32 in 1975 and finally 64 in 1985. Until 1975, only one team per conference was represented. Today, a Selection Committee "seeds" 31 *automatic bids* (teams that finished in 1st place in their conference) and 34 *at-large selections* (other teams chosen based on their records) (32 of each for the women's tournament). Since the number of conferences receiving automatic bids increased to 31 in 2001, to reduce the field from 65 teams (31 + 34 at-large) to 64, the NCAA holds a "tournament in-play" game the day before the start of the tournament between champions of two of the lower-ranked conferences so only one moves into the field of 64 as a #16 seed. The teams that are selected, and sometimes more importantly who they will play and where, are decided behind closed doors over the weekend before the pairings are announced.

The seeding process is controversial, involving difficult decision-making by the committee. In the past, the committee looked to the Associated Press (AP) and USA Today/CNN polls (ranking the top 25 college teams and released weekly on Mondays of the regular season) for assistance. However, in recent years greater parity among colleges produced many different teams that laid claim to the top rankings throughout the season, making the job of deciding which teams are truly better more difficult. Since the tournament is a single-elimination contest, seedings are very important — the higher a team is seeded, the easier its first round games are, and the more likely it is to advance.

The 64 teams actually battle it out in 4 regional groups of 16: West Regional, Midwest Regional, East Regional and Southeast Regional. (For the women's tournament, the regions are the Mideast, Midwest, West and East.) Teams are seeded #1-#16 in each region, and #1 plays #16, #2 vs. #15, #3 vs. #14, etc. (See sample *brackets* in **Fig. 27**) The games take place at 8 neutral sites for the first round, which is followed by a second round, regional semifinals and regional finals, culminating in the *Final Four* which brings together the champions of each region. The 2 winners of the Final Four semifinals square off for the championship on a Monday night, usually the first week of April. Since the entire tournament lasts nearly 3 weeks during which it takes over the sports world, it has been dubbed *"March Madness."* CBS will pay $6B over 11 years ($545M a year) to broadcast the tournament through 2013.

OFFICE POOLS
However difficult, the final decisions of the Selection Committee are revealed on the Sunday evening before the tournament commences in mid-March. The tournament begins at 9:00 am EST Thursday of the same week, so during the 3 days between the announcement of the pairings and the start of March Madness (also called "The Big Dance"), offices and assorted groups of friends around the nation frantically place their picks in pools.

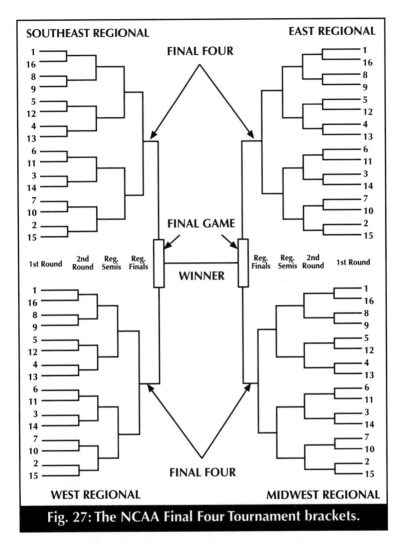

SOUTHEAST REGIONAL

EAST REGIONAL

FINAL FOUR

1
16
8
9
5
12
4
13
6
11
3
14
7
10
2
15

1
16
8
9
5
12
4
13
6
11
3
14
7
10
2
15

1st Round   2nd Round   Reg. Semis   Reg. Finals

Reg. Finals   Reg. Semis   2nd Round   1st Round

FINAL GAME

WINNER

1
16
8
9
5
12
4
13
6
11
3
14
7
10
2
15

1
16
8
9
5
12
4
13
6
11
3
14
7
10
2
15

FINAL FOUR

WEST REGIONAL

MIDWEST REGIONAL

Fig. 27: The NCAA Final Four Tournament brackets.

To run a pool, 2 or more people compete on who can best guess the winners of the tournament. Fill in the name of each team you think will advance to the next round on the form provided in the newspaper when the pairings are announced. One person should run the pool and collect everyone's picks, keeping them posted at the end of each round on how they are faring. Here are some variations on how to calculate points (the winner accumulates the most) — though you can easily develop variations of your own:

- Simple Pool — receive one point for each correct choice.

- Increasing Points Pool — receive 1 point for each correct first round pick, 2 points for each correct second round pick, 3 for each correct regional semifinal pick, 4 for each correct regional final winner, 5 for each correct Final Four semifinal winner and 6 points for the correct champion.

- Upset Pool — this pool can be the most fun. An *upset* is when a team seeded lower upsets a team seeded higher (e.g., #15 beats #2 in the First Round, and it does happen!). The points are calculated as in the Increasing Points Pool, plus points are given for the seed differential of every upset. For example, if you correctly picked that #15 would beat #2 in the First Round, you get 1 point for a correct pick PLUS 13 points for the upset (15-2). This pool should also reward every correct Final Four pick with 5 bonus points to encourage participants to choose only realistic upsets.

NIT

The *National Invitational Tournament*, first held in 1938 when the Metropolitan Basketball Writers of New York sponsored it, is the oldest college postseason tournament. Today, the *NIT* takes place at the same time as the NCAA tournament, starting one day earlier and ending the Wednesday preceding the Final Four weekend at Madison Square Garden. The best Division I teams that were not selected to the NCAA tournament and the best Division II teams are chosen by a committee to fill the 32 available berths in the NIT (for both men and women). Today's rules prevent one team from winning both the NCAA and NIT tournaments, but in 1950 City College of New York (*CCNY*) accomplished the feat. The NIT also sponsors an unrelated pre-season invitational tournament in mid-November that showcases 16 of the top-ranked college teams and kicks off the college season.

INDIVIDUAL & TEAM STATISTICS

Points (PTS): 2 are awarded for each *field goal*, 1 for each *free-throw* and 3 for every *3-point shot*.

Scoring Average or *Points-Per-Game* (PPG): total number of points scored by a player during the season divided by the number of games played. The top *NBA* scorers average between 25-30 points-per-game.

Field Goal Percentage (FG%): the number of successful field goals divided by the number of attempted field goals for a player or a team. A calculation is done every *quarter* for both teams — not surprisingly, the team with the lower percentage is usually behind. A team is shooting well if it has a FG% over 50%. Players who take *inside* shots can have a FG% as high as 60%, while most *outside shooters* make less than 50% of their shots.

Three-Point Field Goal Percentage (3-PT%): the same as the field goal percentage but calculated only for 3-point shots.

Free-Throw Percentage (FT%): the number of successful free-throws divided by the number of attempted free-throws for a player or team. It is important to a team looking to intentionally foul its opponent — it seeks out the player with the lowest percentage because he is more likely to miss the free-throws. An NBA team will have a FT% of around 75%, while college teams fare worse at the line, shooting around 65%. A good NBA free-throw shooter can complete 85% or more of his attempts.

Assists (A): credited to a player whose pass to a teammate directly leads to a field goal. The scorer must move immediately toward the *basket* for the passer to be credited with an assist. The all-time best players average about 13 in a game, while the record is 30.

Bench Scoring: a percentage or total number of points scored by players other than the *starting lineup*, which shows the offensive strength of a team's *bench*.

Defensive Rebounds (DR): the number of rebounds a player or team has on the defensive end of the *court*.

Offensive Rebounds (OR): the number of rebounds a player or team has on its offensive end of the court. These are far less common than defensive rebounds. A team with more of these is more aggressive and more likely to control its own missed shots and score.

Total Rebounds (TR): OR plus DR for a player or team. This statistic has been compiled since 1951. A distinction between OR and DR has only been made since 1973-74.

Steals: when a defensive player gets the ball away from an opponent who controls it. Since players are relatively adept at controlling the ball, steals are hard to get — the highest number in a single game was 11 while the highest average per game is less than 3.

Turnovers: the number of times a team loses *possession* of the ball without taking a shot or without having the other team steal the ball, usually as the result of a *floor violation* or a bad pass that is intercepted or goes *out of bounds*. The team with the higher total is more likely to lose the game and a good defense will cause the offense to commit more of these.

Blocked shots: the number of times a player or team prevents an opponent's field goal attempt by deflecting it with a hand. A player with the ability to block shots can frustrate an offense. These are also rare, with the highest per game average between 3 and 4, although there were 17 by one player in a 1973 game.

In the next 2 chapters you will learn to decipher statistics in the newspaper and see some of the records held by the most noteworthy professional and college players.

DECIPHERING STATISTICS IN THE NEWSPAPER

Each day during the basketball season, most newspapers print much information about pro and college teams. There are *team standings*, showing how each team is performing in terms of wins and losses, and there are summaries of each game played the previous day called *game summaries* or *box scores*. The labeled examples here will help you learn to read all of these with ease.

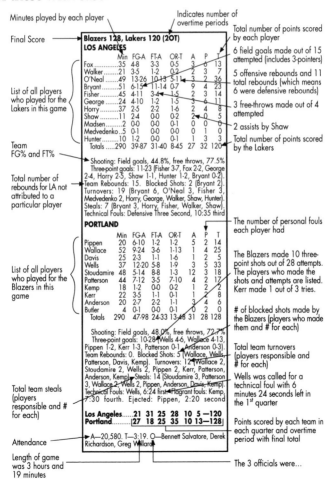

Minutes played by each player

Indicates number of overtime periods

Final Score

Total number of points scored by each player

Blazers 128, Lakers 120 (2OT)
LOS ANGELES

	Min	FG-A	FT-A	OR-T	A	P	T
Fox	35	4-8	3-3	0-5	3	6	13
Walker	21	3-5	1-2	0-2	2	3	7
O'Neal	49	13-26	10-13	5-11	3	2	36
Bryant	51	6-15	11-14	0-7	9	4	23
Fisher	45	4-11	3-4	1-5	2	3	14
George	24	4-10	1-2	1-5	3	6	11
Horry	37	2-5	2-2	1-6	2	4	8
Shaw	11	2-4	0-0	0-2	2	0	5
Madsen	2	0-0	0-0	0-1	0	0	0
Medvedenko	5	0-1	0-0	0-2	0	1	0
Hunter	10	1-2	0-0	0-1	1	3	3
Totals	290	39-87	31-40	8-45	27	32	120

6 field goals made out of 15 attempted (includes 3-pointers)

5 offensive rebounds and 11 total rebounds (which means 6 were defensive rebounds)

3 free-throws made out of 4 attempted

2 assists by Shaw

Total number of points scored by the Lakers

List of all players who played for the Lakers in this game

Team FG% and FT%

Total number of rebounds for LA not attributed to a particular player

Shooting: Field goals, 44.8%, free throws, 77.5%. Three-point goals: 11-23 (Fisher 3-7, Fox 2-2, George 2-4, Horry 2-5, Shaw 1-1, Hunter 1-2, Bryant 0-2). Team Rebounds: 15. Blocked Shots: 2 (Bryant 2). Turnovers: 19 (Bryant 6, O'Neal 3, Fisher 3, Medvedenko 2, Horry, George, Walker, Shaw, Hunter). Steals: 7 (Bryant 3, Horry, Fisher, Walker, Shaw). Technical Fouls: Defensive Three Second, 10:35 third.

PORTLAND

	Min	FG-A	FT-A	OR-T	A	P	T
Pippen	20	6-10	1-2	1-2	5	2	14
Wallace	52	9-24	3-6	1-13	1	4	25
Davis	25	2-3	1-1	1-6	1	2	5
Wells	37	12-20	5-8	1-9	3	5	33
Stoudamire	48	5-14	8-8	1-3	12	3	18
Patterson	44	7-12	3-5	7-10	4	2	17
Kemp	18	1-2	0-0	0-2	1	2	2
Kerr	22	3-5	1-1	0-1	1	4	8
Anderson	20	2-7	2-2	1-1	3	4	6
Butler	4	0-1	0-0	0-1	0	2	0
Totals	290	47-98	24-33	13-48	31	28	128

The number of personal fouls each player had

The Blazers made 10 three-point shots out of 28 attempts. The players who made the shots and attempts are listed. Kerr made 1 out of 3 tries.

# of blocked shots made by the Blazers (players who made them and # for each)

Total team turnovers (players responsible and # for each)

Wells was called for a technical foul with 6 seconds left in the 1st quarter

List of all players who played for the Blazers in this game

Shooting: Field goals, 48.0%, free throws, 72.7%. Three-point goals: 10-28 (Wells 4-6, Wallace 4-13, Pippen 1-2, Kerr 1-3, Patterson 0-1, Anderson 0-3). Team Rebounds: 0. Blocked Shots: 2 (Wallace, Wells, Patterson, Davis, Kemp). Turnovers: 12 (Wallace 2, Stoudamire 2, Wells 2, Pippen 2, Kerr, Patterson, Anderson, Kemp). Steals: 14 (Stoudamire 3, Patterson 3, Wallace 2, Wells 2, Pippen, Anderson, Davis, Kemp). Technical Fouls: Wells, 6:24 first. Flagrant fouls: Kemp, 7:30 fourth. Ejected: Pippen, 2:20 second

Total team steals (players responsible and # for each)

Los Angeles	21	31	25	28	10	5 —120
Portland	27	18	25	35	10	13—128

Points scored by each team in each quarter and overtime period with final total

A—20,580. T—3:19. O—Bennett Salvatore, Derek Richardson, Greg Willard.

Attendance

Length of game was 3 hours and 19 minutes

The 3 officials were...

87

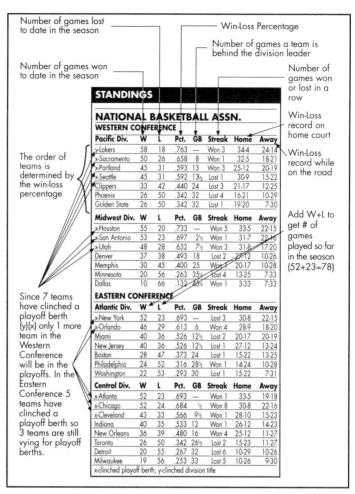

Number of games lost to date in the season

Win-Loss Percentage

Number of games a team is behind the division leader

Number of games won to date in the season

Number of games won or lost in a row

Win-Loss record on home court

The order of teams is determined by the win-loss percentage

Win-Loss record while on the road

Add W+L to get # of games played so far in the season (52+23=78)

Since 7 teams have clinched a playoff berth (y)(x) only 1 more team in the Western Conference will be in the playoffs. In the Eastern Conference 5 teams have clinched a playoff berth so 3 teams are still vying for playoff berths.

STANDINGS

NATIONAL BASKETBALL ASSN.

WESTERN CONFERENCE

Pacific Div.	W	L	Pct.	GB	Streak	Home	Away
y-Lakers	58	18	.763	—	Won 3	34-4	24-14
x-Sacramento	50	26	.658	8	Won 1	32-5	18-21
x-Portland	45	31	.593	13	Won 3	25-12	20-19
x-Seattle	45	31	.592	13½	Lost 1	30-9	15-22
Clippers	33	42	.440	24	Lost 3	21-17	12-25
Phoenix	26	50	.342	32	Lost 4	16-21	10-29
Golden State	26	50	.342	32	Lost 1	19-20	7-30

Midwest Div.	W	L	Pct.	GB	Streak	Home	Away
x-Houston	55	20	.733	—	Won 5	33-5	22-15
x-San Antonio	53	23	.697	2½	Won 1	31-7	22-16
x-Utah	48	28	.632	7½	Won 3	31-8	17-20
Denver	37	38	.493	18	Lost 2	27-12	10-26
Memphis	30	45	.400	25	Won 1	20-17	10-28
Minnesota	20	56	.263	35½	Lost 4	13-25	7-33
Dallas	10	66	.132	45½	Won 1	3-33	7-33

EASTERN CONFERENCE

Atlantic Div.	W	L	Pct.	GB	Streak	Home	Away
x-New York	52	23	.693	—	Lost 3	30-8	22-15
x-Orlando	46	29	.613	6	Won 4	28-9	18-20
Miami	40	36	.526	12½	Won 1	20-17	20-19
New Jersey	40	36	.526	12½	Lost 1	27-12	13-24
Boston	28	47	.373	24	Lost 1	15-22	13-25
Philadelphia	24	52	.316	28½	Won 1	14-24	10-28
Washington	22	53	.293	30	Lost 1	15-22	7-31

Central Div.	W	L	Pct.	GB	Streak	Home	Away
x-Atlanta	52	23	.693	—	Won 1	33-5	19-18
x-Chicago	52	24	.684	½	Won 8	30-8	22-16
x-Cleveland	43	33	.566	9½	Won 1	28-10	15-23
Indiana	40	35	.533	12	Won 1	26-12	14-23
New Orleans	36	39	.480	16	Won 4	25-12	11-27
Toronto	26	50	.342	26½	Lost 2	15-23	11-27
Detroit	20	55	.267	32	Lost 6	10-29	10-26
Milwaukee	19	56	.253	33	Lost 5	10-26	9-30

x-clinched playoff berth; y-clinched division title

Sometimes college scores are reported in this way to conserve space:

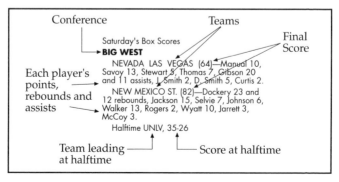

Conference

Teams

Final Score

Saturday's Box Scores
BIG WEST

NEVADA LAS VEGAS (64)—Manual 10, Savoy 13, Stewart 5, Thomas 7, Gibson 20 and 11 assists, L Smith 2, D. Smith 5, Curtis 2.

NEW MEXICO ST. (82)—Dockery 23 and 12 rebounds, Jackson 15, Selvie 7, Johnson 6, Walker 13, Rogers 2, Wyatt 10, Jarrett 3, McCoy 3.

Halftime UNLV, 35-26

Each player's points, rebounds and assists

Team leading at halftime

Score at halftime

NBA & COLLEGE RECORDS

(*=player is still active; statistics current through end of 2001-02 Season)

PROFESSIONAL SCORING LEADERS

All-Time Career Scoring Leaders (NBA only)

Player	Points	Years
Abdul-Jabbar, Kareem	38,387	1969-89
Malone, Karl*	34,707	1985-02
Chamberlain, Wilt	31,419	1959-73
Jordan, Michael*	30,652	1984-02
Malone, Moses	27,409	1976-95
Hayes, Elvin	27,313	1968-84
Olajuwon, Hakeem*	26,946	1984-02
Robertson, Oscar	26,710	1960-74
Wilkins, Dominique	26,668	1982-97
Havlicek, John	26,395	1962-78
English, Alex	25,613	1976-91

All-Time Points Per Game (PPG) Leaders

Player	PPG	Years
Jordan, Michael*	31.0	1984-02
Chamberlain, Wilt	30.1	1959-73
O'Neal, Shaquille *	27.6	1992-02
Baylor, Elgin	27.4	1958-72
West, Jerry	27.0	1960-74
Iverson, Allen*	26.9	1996-02

Most Seasons Leading the League in Scoring

Player	#Seasons	Years
Jordan, Michael*	10	1986-93, 1995-98
Chamberlain, Wilt	7	1959-66

Most Points in a Single Season

Player	Points	Season	Player	Points	Season
Chamberlain, Wilt	4,029	1961-62	Jordan, Michael*	2,868	1987-88
Chamberlain, Wilt	3,586	1962-63	McAdoo, Bob	2,831	1974-75
Jordan, Michael*	3,041	1986-87	Barry, Rick	2,775	1966-67
Chamberlain, Wilt	3,033	1960-61	Jordan, Michael*	2,753	1989-90
Chamberlain, Wilt	2,948	1963-64	Baylor, Elgin	2,719	1962-63

Most Points in a Single Game

Player	Points	Date	Player	Points	Date
Chamberlain, Wilt	100	3/2/62	Chamberlain, Wilt	72	11/3/62
Chamberlain, Wilt	78	12/8/61	Baylor, Elgin	71	11/15/60
Chamberlain, Wilt	73	1/13/62	Robinson, David*	71	4/24/94
Chamberlain, Wilt	73	11/16/62	Chamberlain, Wilt	70	3/10/63
Thompson, David	73	4/9/78	Jordan, Michael*	69	3/28/90

THREE-POINT SHOOTING

Most Career 3-Point Field Goals (only calculated since 1979-80)

Player	3-PT FGs	Years
Miller, Reggie*	2,217	1987-02

Most 3-Point Field Goals in a Single Season

Player	3-PT FGs	Season
Scott, Dennis	267	1995-96
McCloud, George*	257	1995-96

FREE-THROW SHOOTING

Highest Career Free-Throw Percentage (min. 1,200 FTs made)

Player	%	Years
Price, Mark	.904	1986-99
Barry, Rick	.900	1965-80
Murphy, Calvin	.892	1970-83
Skiles, Scott	.889	1979-96

ASSISTS

Most Career Assists

Player	Assists	Years
Stockton, John*	15,177	1984-02
Johnson, Magic	10,141	1979-92, 1995-96
Robertson, Oscar	9,887	1960-74
Jackson, Mark*	9,840	1987-02
Thomas, Isiah	9,061	1986-94

Most Assists in a Single Season

Player	Assists	Season
Stockton, John*	1,164	1990-91
Stockton, John*	1,134	1989-90
Stockton, John*	1,128	1987-88
Stockton, John*	1,126	1991-92
Thomas, Isiah	1,123	1984-85

REBOUNDS (compiled only since 1951)

Most Career Rebounds (includes ABA)

Player	Rebounds	Years
Chamberlain, Wilt	23,924	1959-73
Russell, Bill	21,620	1956-69
Malone, Moses	17,834	1976-95
Abdul-Jabbar, Kareem	17,440	1969-89
Gilmore, Artis	16,330	1971-88

Most Rebounds in a Single Game

Player	Rebounds	Date
Chamberlain, Wilt	55	11/24/60
Russell, Bill	51	2/5/60

STEALS (compiled only since 1973-74)

Most Career Steals

Player	Steals	Years
Stockton, John*	3,128	1978-02

Most Steals in a Single Season

Player	Steals	Season
Robertson, Alvin	301	1985-86

BLOCKED SHOTS (compiled only since 1973-74)

Most Career Blocked Shots

Player	Blocks	Years
Olajuwon, Hakeem*	3,830	1982-02
Abdul-Jabbar, Kareem	3,189	1973-89

Most Blocked Shots in a Single Season

Player	Points	Season
Eaton, Mark	456	1984-85
Bol, Manute	397	1985-86
Smith, Elmore	393	1973-74

Most Blocked Shots in a Single Game

Player	Blocks	Dates
Smith, Elmore	17	10/28/73
Bol, Manute	15	1/25/86 and 2/26/87
O'Neal, Shaquille*	15	11/20/93

COLLEGE SCORING AND ASSIST LEADERS

Most Points in a Single Game

Player	Points	Division	Date
Francis, Clarence "Bevo"	113	Div. II	2/2/54
Selvy, Frank	100	Div. I	2/13/54
Bradshaw, Kevin	72	Div. I	1/5/91

Most Points in a Single Season

Player	Points	Division	Season
Maravich, Pete	1,381	Div. I	1969-70

Most Career Points

Player	Points	Division	Years
Pierce, John	4,260	Div. II	1990-94
Grant, Travis "Machine Gun"	4,045	Div. II	1969-72
Hutcheson, Philip	4,045	Div. II	1986-90
Maravich, Pete	3,667	Div. I	1968-70

Most Career Assists

Player	Points	Division	Years
Hurley, Bobby	1,076	Div. I	1990-93

GREAT TEAMS & DYNASTIES

HALL OF FAME TEAMS

Original Celtics: created in a tough New York City neighborhood in 1914, they were considered the greatest of the early pro teams. They reluctantly joined the *ABL* when it was formed in 1925 only after they faced bankruptcy when other teams refused to play them. Over a 10-year period they traveled through 13 states, winning 1,320 games while losing only 66. They are credited with inventing some of the most creative moves still used today (e.g., *pivot* plays, switching defenses).

Harlem Globetrotters: This all-black team, born in 1926, was the vision of Abe Saperstein, its Jewish immigrant *coach*, who saw great potential in the hard-working players he originally brought together to play serious games. The team turned to entertaining with trick shots, fancy passes and dribbling stunts that audiences seemed to enjoy more. They chose their name to announce they were black (they were really from Chicago) and to make people think they had traveled extensively. The team still exists, amusing fans around the world and acting as goodwill ambassadors for basketball.

The N.Y. Renaissance (*Rens*): Considered the best basketball team in the U.S. between 1932-1936, they amassed an 88-game win streak (1934) and an overall *record* of 473-49. This all-black team traveled for 4 months a year, usually sleeping on the team bus as hotels refused to accommodate them. Organized in Harlem in 1922, the team lasted 27 years, often playing 2 or 3 games a day.

NBA TEAMS

Boston Celtics: They still hold the record for the most *NBA* titles (16), won from 1957 to date (1957, 1959-66, 1968-69, 1974, 1976, 1981, 1984, 1986) and the most consecutive titles (8) in their 19 appearances at the NBA *Finals*. Defense and clever passing was their trademark.

Chicago Bulls: The 1st team to win 3 consecutive NBA titles since the 1960s and 6 in 8 years, they were led to victory by *Michael Jordan* and coach *Phil Jackson*. The only years the Bulls were denied were during Jordan's temporary retirement from October 1993-October 1995. The team reached the *Eastern Conference* Finals even in his absence, then won 3 more titles in 1996, 1997 and 1998 when he returned.

Minneapolis/Los Angeles Lakers: This *franchise* has been a winner since the first days of the NBA — with 6 trips to the Finals and 5 NBA titles (1949, 1950, 1952-54) while still in Minneapolis, then 9 more titles (1972, 1979, 1981, 1985, 1987, 1988, 2000, 2001 and 2002) in 21 trips to the Finals from L.A. Their 33-game winning streak in 1971-72 is still a record. Under coach *Pat Riley*, they dominated the 1980s and coach Phil Jackson unified the team beginning in 1999.

COLLEGE TEAMS

CCNY (City College of N.Y.): Although known more as an academic than an athletic college, CCNY's basketball teams were remarkable (a 36-4 record from 1922-25 and a 43-3 record from 1931-34). It is the only team to win both the *NCAA Tournament* and *NIT* in one year (1950) to be crowned undisputed college champion. Unfortunately, most of that team's members were involved in 1950's *point-shaving* scandal (where players at several colleges accepted bribes to win games by less than the *point spread*) which rocked the college and pro sport for years with allegations of crookedness.

Duke University Blue Devils: In an incredible 16-year stretch from 1986-2002, coach *Mike Krzyzewski* brought them to the *Final Four* 9 times, the final game 7 times and won 3 titles (1991, 1992 and 2001). They are still tied with UNLV (37-2 in 1987) for the most wins in a single season (37-3 in 1986 and 37-2 in 1999). Much of the team's perennial success stems from Coach K's ability to recruit young stars and keep them from graduating early.

Indiana University Hoosiers: the entire state of Indiana seems to participate in "Hoosier Hysteria." The team has won 5 NCAA titles (2nd to *UCLA*), 3 under coach *Bobby Knight* (1976, 1981 and 1987). In his 29 years there, Knight led them to 11 Big 10 titles, 18 NCAA Tournaments, 5 Final Four appearances and 1 NIT title. His Indiana teams had 19 seasons with 20 or more wins while amassing a .737 *winning percentage*.

UCLA (University of California at Los Angeles) Bruins: Under coach *John Wooden* the Bruins won a record 10 NCAA championships (7 consecutive) from 1964-75. They had a 3-year, 88-game winning streak (1971-74), an unprecedented 38-straight wins in NCAA Tournament play and went undefeated 4 seasons (1963-64, 1966-67, 1971-73). It was the first team to use a *full-court press* successfully.

HALL OF FAME

First conceived as a shrine to the game's founder *Dr. James Naismith* when he died in 1939, The Naismith Memorial Basketball *Hall of Fame* first opened on February 18, 1968 in Springfield, Massachusetts (although its first elections had been held nearly a decade earlier in 1959!). Its original site on the Springfield College campus proved inadequate so a modernized three-story complex on the Connecticut River (still in Springfield) became its new home in 1985. A $103 million project doubled its size with a state-of-the-art facility in 2002. Photos, memorabilia and movies honor basketball greats at every level — high school, college, Olympic and professional — and the new hall allows visitors to participate with interactive exhibits.

Individuals are nominated on an annual basis in one of 4 categories: player (5 years after retirement), *coach* (5 years after retirement or after 25 years in the profession if still active), *referee* (5 years after retirement or after 25 years in the profession if still active) and contributor (at any time). The Honors Committee, comprised of 24 members representing many facets of basketball, votes; a minimum of 18 votes is required for induction. Five members are selected annually out of 20+ finalists. They are elected in the spring and enshrined in a fall ceremony later in the same year.

Only two individuals, *John Wooden* and Lenny Wilkens, have been selected twice, first as players (1960 and 1989 respectively) and then as coaches (1972 and 1998). Bill Bradley was inducted when he was a U.S. Senator in 1982. In addition to the 246 individuals enshrined through 2002, 5 teams have been selected: the First Team to play in 1891, the *Original Celtics*, the Buffalo Germans, the *New York Renaissance* (*Rens*), and the *Harlem Globetrotters*.

PERSONALITIES: PAST & PRESENT

It has been said that *Dr. J* saved the NBA, *Magic Johnson* and *Larry Bird* built the league, and *Michael Jordan* polished it. The biographies in this chapter are meant to provide an overview of these and many more of basketball's personalities. Some of its past superstars, potential future stars, *coaches*, analysts and commentators, at both the college and professional level, were chosen. Many personalities have graced the game over the last century, but limited space prevents us from mentioning them all. Please do not be disappointed if your favorites are not here. The *statistics* in this section are current through the end of the 2001-02 season and this key will help you understand the abbreviations in the entries below:

> A=Active, *FG%=field goal percentage*, HF=*Hall of Fame*, H.S.=High School,
> *MVP*=Most Valuable Player, *ppg= points-per-game average*, R=Retired,
> NBA50=Selected one of NBA's 50 Greatest Players of All Time in 1996.

ABDUL-JABBAR, KAREEM (Center, R, HF, NBA50): Born in N.Y. as Ferdinand Lewis Alcindor, he grew up to be "the most dominant player of his lifetime," according to *John Wooden* who coached the 3-time *All-American* at *UCLA* to 3 consecutive *NCAA titles* (1967-69) where Lew was named *Final Four MVP* in each. When the NCAA instituted a no-*dunk* rule to stop this 7'2" giant, it only made him more creative offensively as he developed the unstoppable *skyhook*, a reliable *hook shot* launched from high above any other player on the *court*. This unselfish player, who was the 1st overall *pick* in the 1969 *draft*, started as *Rookie of the Year* and went on to an incredible 20-year NBA career with the Milwaukee Bucks and *L.A. Lakers*. When he retired in 1989 at age 42 he held *records* in nine statistical categories, including *points* scored (38,387), seasons played (20), *playoff* scoring (5,762), MVP awards (6), minutes played (57,446), games played (1,560), *field goals* made and attempted (15,837 of 28,307), and *blocked shots* (3,189). He won 6 championship rings, 4 in his last 8 seasons, and was twice named *NBA Finals* MVP. In 1968, he refused to participate in the Olympics on political grounds and in the early '70s changed his name when he converted to the Muslim faith. Always a very private person, he put off the media until his later years. Since retiring he has kept busy with his 5 children and as president of Kareem Productions (producing movies about the black experience), ESPN commentator, author ("Black Profiles in Courage"), actor (Stephen King wrote a role for him in "The Stand"; "Fletch"; "Airplane"; "The Mighty Ducks"), assistant *coach* (L.A. Clippers 2000), scout/consultant (Indiana Pacers 2001) and with anti-gang, stay in school projects.

AUERBACH, RED (Coach, R, HF): The NBA's most hated and respected *coach* is best known for the cigar he lit after each *Boston Celtics* victory, a ritual symbolic of his defiant personality. During his 50+-year tenure with the Celtics both as coach and member of executive management, the team won a *record* 16 championships, including a record 8 consecutive and 9 out of 10 with him as coach from 1957-1966. Incredibly he never had a losing season in his 20-year coaching career, accumulating a 1,037-548 *record*. The *"Coach of the Year"* award he won in 1965 is now named after him. This success and the advent of televised games brought his behavior into the limelight — the constant stamping of his feet, shouting at *officials* and *technical fouls* led to frequent ejections and fines. He helped break the color barrier in basketball when he selected Chuck Cooper (the 1st black player to join the NBA) in the 1950 *draft* and again when he appointed *Bill Russell* his successor (the NBA's 1st black coach) in 1966. Auerbach has served as coach, general manager or president of an NBA team since the league's inception in 1946. He is the author of 5 basketball books.

BARKLEY, CHARLES (Forward, R, NBA50): (**Photo** on p. 32) Born anemic and raised by a poor, single mother, his H.S. coach called the shy, quiet teenager "average." At Auburn University he was criticized for being lazy. Yet the "Round Mound of *Rebound*", an overweight 1st-round *draft pick* (5th overall) of the Philadelphia 76ers in 1984, became known as "Sir Charles", an outspoken, funny, quotable, aggressive superstar who is one of only 4 players (with *Kareem Abdul-Jabbar*, *Wilt Chamberlain* and *Elgin Baylor*) to amass over 20,000 *points*, 12,000 rebounds and 3,500 *assists* in his 16-year career. The year his tumultuous relationship with the 76ers ended in a trade, a liberated Barkley led the Phoenix Suns to a near *upset* of the defending champion *Chicago Bulls* in the *playoffs* and was named league *MVP* (1992-93). He had another shot at a *title* when traded to the talented Houston Rockets in 1996, but they never made it back to the NBA *Finals* and he retired prematurely with a ruptured leg tendon in 1999. This 12-time *All-Star* and member of two Olympic *Dream Teams* (1992, 1996) also made headlines in scuffles with fans. So outspoken that he was once criticized for having a big mouth, Barkley has received rave reviews as an analyst for TNT's unscripted "Halftime Report" since 2000 and his likeability index has soared. He still works out diligently preparing for a possible comeback to join good friend *Michael Jordan*, while his desire to be an influential black leader has led him to consider running as the Republican candidate for governor of Alabama. An intensely private person, especially when it comes to his 13-year marriage or teenage daughter, he keeps counsel with a small group of loyal friends that includes Tiger Woods. Barkley is an avid golfer who names boxing legend Muhammad Ali as his idol.

BAYLOR, ELGIN (Forward, R, HF, NBA50): A successful mix of agility and muscle made "the man of a thousand moves" a great scorer and powerful *rebounder*. A twitch of the head easily identified this All-American out of Seattle University picked 1ˢᵗ in the 1958 *draft* by the *Minneapolis Lakers*. His 1ˢᵗ year in the NBA he was named *Rookie of the Year* and co-*MVP* of the *All-Star Game*. He spent his entire 14-year career with the *Lakers,* moving to L.A. with the team in 1960 where he combined efforts with *Jerry West* in what was then considered the best tandem in NBA history. Though he led them to 8 NBA *Finals*, Baylor never won a championship. Before *Wilt Chamberlain*, it was Baylor who set and broke the record for most *points* in a single game (63, 64 and 71). Despite nagging knee problems since 1964, his illustrious career continued through 1971, when he retired as the Lakers' all-time leading scorer (23,149 points in just 846 games). Baylor coached the New Orleans Jazz for 2 years until 1979. Since 1986 he has been the general manager of the L.A. Clippers, one of the worst *franchises* in NBA history.

BIRD, LARRY (Forward, R, HF, NBA50): (**Photo** on p. 27): One of the players responsible for revitalizing the NBA, he actually agonized over his career decision — whether to play ball or be a gas station attendant. He chose the NBA, mastering the no-look *pass*, game-winning shot and in-traffic *rebound*. As a H.S. senior in French Lick, Indiana, he was recruited by a Florida college, but stayed home because he was too terrified to get on a plane. In fact, he was too awed to attend Indiana State University until after a few months at a community college. Always an intensely private person, he became wary of the media when he was misquoted early in his difficult personal life (his father committed suicide, a brief marriage ended in divorce and his ex-wife filed a paternity suit, all before 1976). The *Boston Celtics* were so convinced of his talent they used a 1ˢᵗ *round draft pick* to select him in his junior year, though he refused to leave college early. During his 13-year career he was *Rookie of the Year* (1979-80), 3-time league *MVP*, 12-time *All-Star*, twice NBA *Finals* MVP, and a *Dream Team* gold medallist. He led one of the greatest front lines in NBA history (with Robert Parish and Kevin McHale), earning 3 NBA *titles* while appearing in 5 Finals during the 1980s. He finished his illustrious career 11ᵗʰ all-time in scoring, 8ᵗʰ in *steals*, 4ᵗʰ in *free-throw percentage*, 4ᵗʰ in *3-pointers* made (649) and 2ⁿᵈ only to *Magic Johnson* in career *triple-doubles* (59). When a bad back forced him to retire in 1992, he became a Celtics special assistant for 5 years. In 1998, Bird was named *Coach of the Year* his 1ˢᵗ season with the Indiana Pacers and 2 years later led them to the NBA Finals before retiring from coaching.

BRYANT, KOBE (Guard, A) This quick, high-flying guard is fluent in Italian and is the son of former NBA player Joe "Jellybean" Bryant. Named for a type of beef, Kobe jumped straight into the NBA from Lower Merion High School (also co-author Ominsky's alma mater!) to become the youngest player (18 yrs./5 mos./5 days) to start in an NBA game. Despite his youth and lack of college experience, Kobe was the 13ᵗʰ *pick* in the 1996 *draft* (traded by Charlotte Hornets to *L.A. Lakers*) and enjoyed an impressive *rookie* season, scoring in double figures 25 times and winning the 1996-97 *All-Star* Weekend's *Slam Dunk* Contest. In his 2nd season he became the youngest-ever All-Star starter, posting a team-high 18 *points* and 6 *rebounds*. By his 6th season, Kobe was one of the best in the league (3rd-highest scoring average) and had matured into a leader as Lakers' co-*captain*. A highly publicized feud with *Shaquille O'Neal* seemed overblown as the two led their team, under the tutelage of *coach Phil Jackson*, to 3 straight NBA championships (2000, 2001, 2002). In 2001, Kobe married a model he met on a video shoot, presenting Vanessa with a 7-carat engagement ring while she was still in H.S. Considering Kobe is still in his early 20s, many believe he is the heir-apparent to *Michael Jordan*.

CARTER, VINCE (Forward, A): In 1998, his junior year at North Carolina, he was drafted 5th and immediately traded to the Toronto Raptors. Over the next few years, "Showtime" developed into a human highlight film with high-flying acrobatics reminiscent of the early *Michael Jordan* years. Praised for an all-around power game and the speed and agility to alternate between *forward* and *guard*, Carter won *Rookie of the Year* honors in 1999 and became a 3-time leading *All-Star* vote-getter. He is credited with some of history's most famous *dunks*, including jumping over a standing 7'2" French center during the Olympics. This gold medallist (2000) plays the saxophone, was a drum major and a member of the marching band in H.S., and even received a music scholarship offer. Though charming both on and off the court, Carter breached a contract with Puma in favor of a $30 million one with Nike. After the 2001 *playoffs*, he signed a 6-year $94 million contract extension, the richest contract in Canadian sports history.

CHAMBERLAIN, WILT (Center, R, HF, NBA50): "Wilt the Stilt" was a 7'1" powerhouse who broke every NBA scoring record, but he was also a moody, introspective player who often missed practice and created tensions with *coaches* and teammates. In anticipation of his NBA arrival, NBC expanded its game coverage to both Saturday and Sunday. After leaving the University of Kansas as a junior and playing with the *Harlem Globetrotters* for a year, Wilt joined the NBA's Philadelphia (later San Francisco) Warriors in 1959 and averaged an impressive 37.6 *ppg* in his *rookie* season. Once he was named *Rookie of the Year*, Wilt announced his retirement claiming he had nothing left to prove, and that he preferred to be a successful businessman appreciated for his brains. It was this type of independent and arrogant behavior that caused critics to call him selfish, instead of admiring his accomplishments. Still, his Philadelphia 76ers (traded in 1964) was the only team able to break the *Boston Celtics'* championship winning streak when they took the *title* in 1967. He joined the *L.A. Lakers* in 1968, and in 1971-72 led them to 33 consecutive victories (still a *record*) and an NBA title.

Wilt won the scoring title 7 years in a row and led the NBA in *rebounding* 11 times. He averaged over 50 ppg one season (1961-62) and scored an incredible 100 points in one game! Had he not been such a poor *free-throw shooter* (a career average of 51%) he would have been even more devastating. A perennial *All-Star*, he was voted league *MVP* 4 times and NBA *Finals* MVP once. Upon retiring, he became a restauranteur, pro volleyball player, and author. He shocked the public when he bragged about sleeping with over 20,000 women in his autobiography. He published another controversial book on the sad state of sports in 1997. Wilt died of heart failure in 1999 at age 63.

COUSY, BOB (Guard, R, HF, NBA50): "Cooz", an All-American from Holy Cross College, was one of the most gifted ball handlers in NBA history, *dribbling* well with either hand or behind his back, and even more adept at *passing* to set up plays for teammates. This "Houdini of the Hardwood" led the NBA in *assists* for 8 consecutive years (1953-60) and was voted league *MVP* in 1957. Though a popular college star, *coach Red Auerbach* thought he was too small and too flashy for the *Boston Celtics*. It was only through a 1950 mini-*expansion draft* drawing held after Cousy's NBA team folded that he landed in Boston. He toned down his passing style and in time Red beamed "There's nobody as good as Cousy — and there never was." Still, Cooz did not win a championship until *Bill Russell* joined the team, and together they amassed 6 *titles*. In his 13-year career Cooz was selected to the All-NBA Team 10 years in a row and participated in 13 *All-Star Games*. When he retired in 1963 he coached at Boston College until 1974.

DUNCAN, TIM (Forward, A) This St. Croix native's original dream was to be an Olympic swimmer (he was a top competitor in the 400 freestyle), but he turned to basketball in the 9th grade after Hurricane Hugo destroyed his island's only training pool. Duncan's exceptional college career at Wake Forest (1st in ACC and 2nd in *NCAA* history with 481 *blocked shots*) culminated in his being named consensus National *Player of the Year* his senior year. The 1st overall *draft pick* in 1997, he went to the San Antonio Spurs where he earned *Rookie of the Year* and *All-Star* honors in his first season. Since then, he has emerged as one of the best *power forwards* and *rebounders* in the NBA. In just his 2nd season he was named 1999 NBA *Finals MVP* as he led the Spurs to an NBA *title*, and in 2002 he won MVP honors for the season as he led the league in *double-doubles*, was 2nd in rebounding and 7th in *ppg*. A very modest man who sports tattoos of a magician and a wizard, Duncan is afraid of heights and sharks, collects knives, and is known for wearing his practice shorts backwards, a trend he started in college.

ERVING, JULIUS (Forward, R, HF, NBA50): Called *"Doctor J"* because of how he "operated" on the court, he went from the University of Massachusetts to the *ABA* for 5 years, then joined the Philadelphia 76ers in 1976 for 11 seasons. Dr. J was the 1st player to make spectacular

99

high-flying acrobatic moves – the *slam dunk* was his trademark – later copied by players like *Michael Jordan*. In the ABA, he led the N.Y. Nets to 2 championships, was voted *MVP* 3 years in a row (1974-76), led the league in scoring 3 times and is largely credited as the reason for the merger of the ABA and NBA. He was also named NBA MVP (1980-81) and led the 76ers to a *title* in 1983. He scored over 1,000 *points* in each of his 16 seasons, and is one of only 3 players to score 30,000+ career points. When he retired in 1987, Erving first distanced himself from the sport, becoming a successful businessman with a Coca-Cola bottling company and a cable TV firm. Fulfilling the urge to return to the game, he became a sports analyst for NBC in 1993 and vice-president of the Orlando Magic in 1997. In 1999, media attention focused on him when he acknowledged being the father of tennis phenom Alexandra Stevenson, and then again a year later, when tragically, his teenage son Cory was found dead. Dr. J will be remembered for stepping forward when the NBA was losing credibility, participating in countless charities and bringing a positive attitude to all he did. Named Sportsman of the Decade (1980s), he is still one of the sport's greatest ambassadors.

HILL, GRANT (Forward, A): A consummate gentleman recognized for tremendous community service, Hill completed a standout college career at *Duke University* that included back-to-back *NCAA championships* (1991, 1992) after which the Detroit Pistons selected him 3rd overall in the 1994 *draft*. He shared *Rookie of the Year* honors with Jason Kidd and became the first *rookie* in *NBA* history to lead in *All-Star* votes. His 2nd season he led the NBA in *triple-doubles* and won the Olympic gold (1996), and by 1999-00 he had raised his scoring average to 25.8 *ppg* (3rd in NBA). Hill was team leader in *points*, *rebounds* and *assists* 3 of his 5 seasons with the Pistons, joining *Elgin Baylor* and *Wilt Chamberlain* as the only players to lead their teams in all 3 categories in at least 3 seasons. The Orlando Magic had great expectations when they acquired Hill in 2000, but he spent the next 2 seasons rehabilitating a broken and then re-injured ankle and his future capabilities remain uncertain. In 1997, Hill signed a 7-year $80-million deal with Fila, the 2nd highest sports endorsement contract to date. His father, Calvin, was an NFL running back and his wife, Tamia, is a 4-time Grammy-nominated R&B recording artist, songwriter and actress.

IVERSON, ALLEN (Guard, A): Easily identified by the signature rows a hairdresser fixes twice a week, this *point guard* likes to shoot and penetrates to the basket with lightning speed. Born to a 15-year old single mother, Iverson's home above the town sewer frequently flooded with sewage. He overcame adversity through sports, becoming Virginia's Player of the Year in both basketball and football (quarterback). Despite some legal run-ins including 4 months in jail, Georgetown *coach* John Thompson recruited him. After just 2 superb

100

college seasons, Iverson was selected 1st in the 1996 NBA *draft* by the Philadelphia 76ers. His 1st season he averaged 23.5 *ppg* (6th in the NBA), 7.5 *assists* and 2.07 *steals*, and became the 2nd youngest player to score 50 *points* in a game on his way to winning *Rookie of the Year*. Accused of selfish play throughout his career for his non-stop shooting, Iverson quieted his critics in 2001 by leading the 76ers to the NBA *Finals*. That year he won his 2nd scoring *title* in 3 years (31.1 ppg – the 1st player since *Michael Jordan* in 1996 to average more than 30 ppg), led the league in steals (2.51 per game), and was named *All-Star MVP* and NBA MVP. Iverson recently decided not to release his controversial rap CD (entitled "Misunderstood", the epitaph he wants on his tombstone), and married his longtime Georgetown girlfriend, continuing to provide financial support to a large extended family and his 2 children. Just when it seemed he was becoming more responsible, Iverson was arrested in July 2002 for threatening 2 men with a gun. Though some still feel his brashness detracts from his accomplishments, consider this: only 7 rookies in NBA history averaged 40 minutes and 20 ppg. Six are *Hall of Famers*; the 7th (and 1st to reach those benchmarks in 27 years) is Iverson.

JACKSON, PHIL (Coach, A): This unconventional *coach* holds a near-monopoly on NBA championships, leading his teams to win 9 of the last 12. The son of evangelical ministers, he meditates daily, listens to the Grateful Dead and uses literature to influence his players. During 13 years as a *forward* for the N.Y. Knicks, he developed a fondness for cigars, which he insists on smoking in private. After a brief stint as a TV commentator, he coached in the *CBA* and was named *Coach of the Year*. Then, in 9 seasons as *Chicago Bulls'* head coach, he guided them to 6 NBA championships (3 straight twice: 1991-93, 1996-98). Many gave *Michael Jordan* the credit, forgetting he had played 5 *ring*-less years before Jackson. After a year hiatus, Jackson joined the *L.A. Lakers*, immediately leading them to 3 straight NBA *titles* (2000-2002) and helping 8-year veteran and superstar *Shaquille O'Neal* to his 1st rings. With his third *three-peat*, Jackson not only tied *Red Auerbach*'s championship record (9), but he became the first coach to lead 2 different teams to 3 consecutive titles. As coach, Jackson boasts the best overall *winning percentage* (.738) and *playoff* winning percentage (.743) in NBA history, and was twice selected NBA *Coach of the Year* (1996, 1997). His spiritual, easy-going nature successfully guided the eccentricities of *Dennis Rodman*, and settled the feuds of Jordan/*Scottie Pippen* and *Kobe Bryant*/Shaq. He spends his summers in Montana riding his Harley in the company of Jeannie Buss (daughter of Lakers' owner Jerry Buss) and is reluctant to sign autographs, preferring the human connection of shaking hands or talking with fans.

JOHNSON, EARVIN "MAGIC" (Guard, R, HF, NBA50): He was simply *Magic* (or Buck or Junior to his friends). Always beaming his famous smile, he infused teamwork into pro basketball, and made the no-look *pass* his signature. At 6'9", he revolutionized the *point guard* position previously reserved for smaller players with his combination of size and unsurpassed *court vision*, inspiring the addition of the *triple-double* to the NBA's *statistics*. When it came to combining scoring, *rebounding*, ball handling and leadership, Magic excelled as no other player had. His decade-long rivalry with *Larry Bird* began in college (when as a sophomore Magic led Michigan State to the *NCAA title* over Bird's team) and aided the NBA's rebirth. Selected 1st in the *draft* as a million dollar *rookie* in 1979, Magic led the *L.A. Lakers* to the championship, scoring 42 *points* while playing every position in the final game. During his 12-year career, he led the team to 9 NBA *Finals* and 5 titles, was named *Finals* MVP and league MVP 3 times each, was a 12-time *All-Star* and left the NBA in 1991 ranked 1st in *assists* (9,921)—testimony to his unselfish play— and 2nd in *steals* (1,698).

He first retired at the start of the 1991-92 season with the announcement that he was HIV-positive, becoming a spokesman for the disease AIDS. Though retired, fans voted him to the 1992 All-Star Game where he was named MVP, and that summer he won an Olympic gold medal with the *Dream Team*. His brief comeback attempt was fraught with controversy as players grappled with the issue of infectious diseases on the court. He *coached* the Lakers for the last 16 games of the 1993-94 season, then became the team's vice-president when he purchased a 5% interest for $10-$15 million, realizing his dream to own an NBA *franchise*. He relinquished that stake for another comeback in January 1996 and led the Lakers to the *playoffs* before retiring again. Today this father of 3 is a savvy businessman (his empire of movie theatres, shopping centers and restaurants is committed to developing inner city neighborhoods), serves as an executive with the Lakers, tours and plays internationally with other former NBA players as part of the Magic Johnson All-Stars Team, and is even considering a run for mayor of Los Angeles in 2005.

JORDAN, MICHAEL (Guard, A, NBA50): "Air Jordan" defies gravity, soaring toward the basket with his tongue hanging from his mouth. Fans gaze in awe at the perfect basketball player, the most complete package of grace, creativity and athleticism. After being cut from his H.S. team as a sophomore, Jordan quickly became a standout collegiate player at the University of North Carolina, hitting the game-winning shot to win the national championship as a freshman in 1982. After the *Chicago Bulls* chose him 3rd in the 1984 NBA *draft*, Jordan quickly established himself by winning *Rookie of the Year* and then, in 1987-88, *Defensive Player of the Year* and league *MVP* (the 1st of 5 times). In spite of all his individual accomplishments, it took him 7 seasons to win an NBA *title*. Only when *Scottie Pippen* and coach *Phil Jackson* joined the team was Jordan able to lead the Bulls to 6 titles (twice 3 in a row:

1991-93, 1996-98), winning *Finals* MVP honors each time. He has the highest career scoring average of any NBA player (31.0 *ppg*), led the league in scoring a record 10 years (7 consecutive), and led in *steals* 3 times. Jordan is also a 2-time Olympic gold medallist (1984, 1992)

Jordan's surprise retirement in 1993 came after rumors of gambling problems and the bizarre carjacking murder of his father. Pursuing his dream to play major league baseball, he joined the minor league Birmingham Barons but struggled as a hitter (.202 batting average) and missed basketball. When the 11-time *All-Star* returned to the NBA in 1995, he immediately led the Bulls to a record 72-win season and 3 more championships, retiring again in 1998 after hitting the championship-winning shot with 5 seconds left in Game 6. In 1999 he rejoined the league as part-owner of the Washington Wizards but came out of retirement as a player in 2001 to help teach his young players how to win. Jordan is a marketing machine (reportedly earning an average $53 million in endorsements in addition to his $33 million salary each year), and Fortune magazine estimates his impact on the economy to be in the hundreds of millions if not billions of dollars. However, today he is less motivated by endorsements and has kept his vow not to renew contracts as they expire. When he does finally retire, this avid golfer and #1-most-esteemed athlete to kids 12-17 will be remembered for his heart, relentless drive, and ability to single-handedly win a game in its closing minutes.

KNIGHT, BOB (Coach, A, HF): This mercurial college *coach's* legendary career began in 1964 with Army where he coached for 6 years before moving to the *Indiana Hoosiers* for 29 years. His uncanny ability to extract the best from even untalented teams helped him lead Indiana to 11 conference *titles*, 5 *Final Fours*, and 3 national championships. One of the youngest coaches to reach 700 career wins, he also boasts a 98% graduation rate among his 4-year players. Knight has a notoriously bad temper, once throwing a chair onto the court to protest an *official's* call. Eventually, several controversial run-ins with media and players (including his own son who he struck in 1992 for making an error in a game) prompted Indiana to fire this school legend in 2000. Six months later he joined a desperate Texas Tech, taking them to the *NCAA Tournament* for the first time in 6 years.

KRZYZEWSKI, MIKE (Coach, A, HF): (Pronounced Shuh-chef-ski) Known simply as "Coach K", this extremely popular and respected disciple of *Bobby Knight* at Army imprinted his own successful style at *Duke*, leading the Blue Devils to 18 *NCAA* tournaments, 9 *Final Fours* (5 consecutive 1988-92), 6 finals and 3 *titles* (1991, 1992, 2001) while earning 11 *Coach of the Year* honors. Though lured by the NBA, he signed a lifetime contract with Duke in 2001, staying where he is most comfortable and taking an interest in seeing his "kids" graduate (93% do!). He also signed a 15-year $6.6M contract with Nike in 1993. **103**

LESLIE, LISA (Center, A): In 2001, her 5th season in the *WNBA*, Lisa became the league's all-time leading scorer (2,670 *points*), passing former Houston Comets guard Cynthia Cooper (2,537 points) on her way to leading the L.A. Sparks to the 1st championship not won by the Comets in league history, and capturing both *All-Star* and *regular-season MVP* honors. That same year, the Sparks became the first team to remain undefeated at home an entire season (16-0) and went on a record 18-game winning streak, as she finished in the top 3 in *scoring* (19.5 *ppg*), *rebounding* (9.6 per game) and *blocked shots* (2.29 per game). On July 31, 2002 she became the 1st woman to *slam dunk* in a pro game. Growing up, Lisa's single mother worked as a cross-country trucker, leaving her to raise her younger sister in Compton, California. Lisa's cousin taught her basketball when she reached 6-feet in height by the 6th grade, and she received national attention by scoring 101 points in the 1st half of a high school game. One of the most highly recruited players in the nation, she attended the University of Southern California where she earned College *Player of the Year* honors (1994). A 2-time Olympic gold medallist (1996, 2000), Lisa also enjoys a successful career as a model.

MALONE, KARL (Forward, A, NBA50): Though only picked 13th in the 1985 *draft* by the Utah Jazz, "The Mailman" has missed only 7 games in his career and never delivered less than 21.7 *ppg* after his *rookie* year. Malone poses a threat in so many ways: he is able to run the floor, *rebound* and shoot from mid-range. Also, his size and strength make it difficult to *guard* him in the *low post*. This 13-time *All-Star* was twice league *MVP* (1997, 1999) and won 2 Olympic gold medals (1992, 1996). He holds the NBA record for most consecutive seasons scoring 2,000+ *points* (11) and in 2000 became 2nd on the NBA's all-time scoring list (passing *Wilt Chamberlain*). With *John Stockton*, he has led the Jazz to the *playoffs* every year of his career and vows not to retire until he wins an NBA *title*. Malone is active in Special Olympics, owns a Toyota dealership and an Arkansas ranch, enjoys driving both 18-wheelers and Harley motorcycles and sells videos of his workout secrets.

MALONE, MOSES (Center, R, HF, NBA50): This son of a Virginia meat packer never attended college, taught himself the game and became a star through relentless *rebounding* at both ends, winning 6 rebounding titles in 7 years and 3 NBA *MVP* awards. In 1995, he retired 4th in scoring (29,580 *points*), 3rd in rebounding (17,834) and 3rd in career games (1,455) (including his *ABA* statistics). A 12-time NBA *All-Star*, "Old Man Malone" played 21 seasons (19 NBA) for 2 ABA and 7 NBA teams. He considers leading the Philadelphia 76ers with *Julius Erving* to the 1983 NBA *title* while being named *Finals* MVP his greatest personal triumph. He talks little (some mistake his swift rumbling voice for inarticulateness) and compares himself to Columbo.

MARAVICH, PETE (Guard, R, HF, NBA50): Known for his flashy passes, "Pistol Pete" rewrote the *NCAA* record books while at Louisiana State University. This 3-time All-American (1967-70) led in scoring for 3 straight years and still holds the *records* for single-season scoring (1,381 in 1970) and career *points* (3,667 in 83 games), averaging an amazing 44.2 *ppg*. He joined the NBA after his junior year, averaging 24.2 points over his career and playing in 5 *All-Star Games*. His offbeat trademark in the NBA was his inability to keep his socks up. He once said, "I don't want to play 10 years in the NBA and die of a heart attack at age 40." Tragically, that is exactly what he did, collapsing during a pick-up game in 1988 when he was just 40 years old.

MIKAN, GEORGE (Center, R, HF, NBA50): The 1st great *center*, Mikan was told by his H.S. coach he was too tall and big, and therefore too clumsy for the game. This 3-time All-American at DePaul went on to dominate the NBA *record* books, scoring 44 or more *points* in 9 games and 61 points in a 1952 game. Crowds packed arenas as "Mr. Basketball" led the NBA in scoring 3 years in a row, won 5 NBA *titles* in 6 years with the *Minneapolis Lakers* and was voted Top Player of the 1st Half-Century by the Associated Press. As opposing teams searched for a big man to stop him, he forced the NBA to change many of its rules (adding the *goaltending* rule, introducing the *24-second clock*, limiting *team fouls* and widening the *foul lane*). He retired in 1956, becoming the *ABA*'s 1st *Commissioner* in 1967. In the 1990s, while in his 70s he purchased a roller hockey team, handling daily duties like washing mascot suits. His right leg was amputated due to diabetes in 2001.

OLAJUWON, HAKEEM (Center, A, NBA50): Hakeem "the Dream" played soccer in his native Nigeria, not showing his remarkable agility at basketball until age 15. In his 2 years at the University of Houston he led the team to the *NCAA* finals twice and was once named *Final Four MVP* in spite of losing that year. Selected 1st in the 1984 *draft* by the Houston Rockets, he stayed with the team 17 seasons, tying the NBA *record* for most seasons with a single team before being traded to the Toronto Raptors in 2001. An intimidating defensive presence at 7' tall, Olajuwon became the all-time NBA leader in *blocked* shots (3,830). He led the Rockets to back-to-back championships (1994, 1995), winning *Finals* MVP honors both times and garnering NBA MVP and *Defensive Player of the Year* in 1993-94, the 1st player to win all 3 awards in the same season. Olajuwon is also the only player to lead a team in 5 categories: *points*, *assists*, *rebounds*, blocks and *steals*. Becoming an American citizen (1993) enabled him to win the gold with Dream Team III (1996). Olajuwon (whose name means "always on top") credits being a devout Muslim for the patience to await a new owner after a *salary cap* technicality kept him in Houston. The parents of this 12-time *All-Star* consider the sport so violent they have never seen him play in person, watching him win his NBA *titles* on TV.

105

O'NEAL, SHAQUILLE (Center, A, NBA50): Considered by some to be the greatest *center* that ever played the game, "Shaq" left Louisiana State University his junior year to become the Orlando Magic's 1st *draft pick* in 1992 and *Rookie of the Year*. This 7'1", 315-pound center with size 22EEE shoes and thundering *dunks* won an Olympic gold medal (1996) and consistently ranks in the top 10 in *scoring*, *rebounding*, *blocks* and *field goal percentage*, but remains a bad *free-throw* shooter (about 50%). In 1996, this *free agent* signed the then-richest contract in NBA history (7 years, $121 million) with the *L.A. Lakers*, but proved a great value as he led the team to 3 straight NBA championships (2000, 2001, 2002), earning the *Finals MVP* award in all 3. The Lakers quickly offered him an $88.5 million 3-year contract extension. When named league MVP in 2000, Shaq was honored with the highest percentage of 1st place MVP votes in NBA history (99.2%, only 1 vote for *Allen Iverson*). His boyish charm continues to land booming endorsements (estimated at $24 million+ a year) and with a clothing line, a record label, a book, 5 rap albums (one platinum), 2 video games and 6 movies to his name, this embraceable giant is the NBA's marketing king. Shaq's aspirations to become a sheriff led him to join the L.A. police reserves. "Little warrior" (his Islamic name) sports a Superman tattoo on his left bicep, balanced by "The World is Mine" on his right.

RILEY, PAT (Coach, A): With his slicked back hair and Armani suits, "Riles" is one of the NBA's greatest *coaches*. In 20 seasons he failed to make the *playoffs* only once, amassing 16 *division titles*, 8 *Finals* appearances, 4 championships and 1,085 wins (2nd all-time). He sports an incredible .679 *winning percentage* including an unprecedented 13 consecutive seasons of 50+ wins. Riley made his mark coaching the *L.A. Lakers* from 1981-1990 (where he also played *guard* in the '70s) taking them to the NBA Finals 7 times and winning 4 titles, including the NBA's first back-to-back titles in 20 years. In his quest for a 3rd consecutive title, Riley copyrighted the phrase *"three-peat"*, but not until *Phil Jackson's Chicago Bulls* and L.A. Lakers pulled it off did he earn substantial royalties. He then led the N.Y. Knicks from 1991-1995, taking them to their 1st Finals in 20 years in just his 2nd season. He resigned amid controversy to accept a lucrative contract as head coach and part-owner of the Miami Heat and again guided a losing team to a division title in just 2 years, creating an intense rivalry with the Knicks. His versatility is evidenced by 3 *Coach of the Year* awards — with the graceful Lakers (1990), the aggressive Knicks (1993) and the rebuilt Heat (1996). This best-selling author and highly paid motivational speaker uses temper tantrums, Shakespeare and Sun-Tzu quotes to inspire his players.

ROBERTSON, OSCAR (Guard, R, HF): No one knew what to expect when the versatile "Big O" had the ball. A strong jumper with incredible body control, a soft, reliable *shooting touch* and an instinct for *steals*, he could pass, *dribble* and *rebound* as well as he could score. This Indiana native was elected to the National Honor Society, graduating in the top 10% of his H.S. Despite many options he chose the University of Cincinnati's work-training program, but as its 1st black basketball player he suffered many insults. He persevered and was named *Player of the Year* 3 times and broke 14 *NCAA* records (including being the 1st player to lead in scoring 3 years in a row). Joining the NBA's Cincinnati Royals in 1960, he was named *Rookie of the Year* as he averaged 30.5 *ppg* (he is still among all-time scoring leaders), 9.7 *assists* (to lead the NBA, which he did 5 more times) and 10 *rebounds*. In 1964 he was named NBA *MVP*. Only after joining the Milwaukee Bucks and *Kareem-Abdul Jabbar*, however, did he win an NBA *title* (1970-71). An *All-Star* each of his 14 years (3-time MVP), he also won the Olympic gold (1960). Since retiring, he has been active with charities and as a broadcaster, author and entrepreneur.

RODMAN, DENNIS (Forward, R): Although both his sisters were college basketball All-Americans, Rodman did not play organized ball until he was 20 when he left his graveyard shift as an airport janitor, enrolled in junior college, and then transferred to Southeastern Oklahoma State. The Detroit Pistons selected this obscure player in the 2nd *round* (27th *pick*) of the 1986 *draft* and "the Worm" went on to become an integral part of 5 NBA championship teams (Detroit 1989, 1990; *Chicago Bulls* 1996-1998). This legendary rebounder averaged 18.7 per game (the best since *Wilt Chamberlain*'s 19.2 twenty years earlier), led the league in *rebounds* 7 consecutive years and was twice named *Defensive Player of the Year* (1990, 1991). Rodman once confided in Detroit's *coach* Chuck Daly that his strong work ethic and good behavior were unappreciated, so he retooled his image. He soon became better known for headline-making eccentric behavior on and off the court with his ever-changing hair-color, the kicking of a courtside photographer, cross-dressing, a brief marriage to actress Carmen Elektra, a WWWF match against RuPaul, a tryst with Madonna, several movie and TV roles, and hosting wild parties. In stints with the San Antonio Spurs, *L.A. Lakers* and Dallas Mavericks who released him in 2000, Rodman brought with him such distractions that teams today are unwilling to sign him in spite of his interest in returning to the NBA.

RUSSELL, BILL (Center, R, HF, NBA50): Russell was not a prolific scorer (15 *ppg* career), but his *defensive* abilities set him apart. Using a unique combination of height, reflexes and intelligence he became a great *rebounder* and *shot blocker*. He led the University of San Francisco to 55 consecutive victories and 2 *NCAA titles*, then led the *Boston Celtics* to 11 *titles* in 13 years, was named *Player of the Year* 5 times (3 in a row 1961-63) and led the NBA in rebounding 4 times. His great rivalry with *Wilt Chamberlain* touched everything (when Wilt got a $100,000

3-year contract, he asked for $100,001). In 1966, when *Red Auerbach* retired, Russell became the first black *coach* of a professional team in any major sport, leading the Celtics to 2 more titles (1967-68, 1968-69) before retiring. This outspoken advocate of African-American rights was less successful as coach/general manager of the Seattle Supersonics (1973-77) and coach of the Sacramento Kings (1987-88). Though an uncomfortable NBA color analyst for several years, he dabbled with acting, once appearing on the TV show "Miami Vice", and wrote a provocative autobiography "Second Wind." His refusal to sign autographs is legendary.

SMITH, DEAN (Coach, R, HF): In 1997, after 36 seasons coaching the University of North Carolina Tar Heels, the man known for his long, beak-like nose and furrowed brows retired as the winningest *coach* in *NCAA* history. His 879 wins topped Adolph Rupp's longtime record of 876. Along the way Smith had only one losing season (his first), accumulated 27 consecutive 20-win seasons, won more *NCAA Tournament* games than any other coach (65 in 25 appearances), and boasted 30 All-American players including *Michael Jordan* on his rosters. In 11 *Final Four* appearances, he won 2 NCAA titles (1982, 1993) to add to his *NIT title* and Olympic gold medal. Known for his integrity and revered as a father figure by many of his players, Smith is also credited with such innovations as the "four-corner defense" and the "sophisticated motion offense." Also a generous man, he shared his $300,000 a year from Nike with assistant coaches and office staff.

STERN, DAVID (Commissioner, A): A long way from working in his father's deli, Stern is responsible for creating the NBA's international sports and entertainment empire (games air in 43 languages in 210 countries). He started as its outside attorney in 1966 before becoming its first legal counsel. In 1983, when financial difficulties gripped the league, he shrewdly borrowed the NFL's idea of promising players a percentage of the owners' take, allowing the owners to contain labor costs by imposing a *salary cap* based on that percentage. Since becoming its 4th *Commissioner* in 1984, he has astutely encouraged the marketing of the NBA's superstars, a strategy largely credited as the driving force behind the league's popularity. Stern added 6 teams, developed NBA Properties, NBA Entertainment and NBA International divisions, successfully instituted policies and rule changes that broadened the league's appeal, and quadrupled revenues on the way to making the NBA the most widely distributed sports property after the Olympics. In 1997, he launched the *WNBA* with a similar marketing effort. Despite a decline in TV ratings, Stern engineered a $2.64 billion package in 1998. Then, anticipating the decline of network television, he propelled the NBA to become the first major sports league to air the majority of its games on cable stations beginning in 2002, signing a $4.6 billion deal. His greatest challenge remains stabilizing labor strife.

STOCKTON, JOHN (Guard, A, NBA50): This 6'1" graduate of Gonzaga and 2-time Olympic gold medallist (1992, 1996) can *pass, shoot, steal* and play incredible *defense*. Not surprisingly, he is the *NBA*'s all-time leader in both *assists* and steals. In fact, he holds every imaginable assist *record*, including leading the league 9 years in a row (1987-1996, breaking *Bob Cousy*'s record of 8). With *Karl Malone* he is part of the most consistently productive *guard/forward* tandem in the game, bringing the Utah Jazz to the *playoffs* each year they have played together. His terrific passes leave observers scratching their heads in wonderment, while his consistent lack of *turnovers* further frustrates opponents. This 10-time *All-Star* missed only 4 games his first 13 seasons, none since returning from knee surgery in 1997. Stockton is easy to spot on the court, as he still will not wear the long shorts popularized in the 1990s.

VITALE, DICK (Commentator, A): The most outrageous hoops color man ever, "Dicky V" is a bubbly marathon talker who rarely inhales. His unmistakable "awesome, bay-bee" can be heard everywhere — during countless college games on ESPN and ABC, speaking engagements, endorsement appearances, interviews and his weekly radio show. Some critics accuse him of missing defensive subtleties but his exuberant telecasts are memorable — full of phrases like "He's a Diaper Dandy" (a top freshman) or "that shot was Brick City, baby" — as he makes (and keeps) outrageous promises to his fans ("I'll stand on my head if X beats Y"). With one glass eye, this former college and NBA *coach* is one of the friendliest celebrities, spending his own money to mail fans basketballs, books and hats.

WALTON, BILL (Center, R, HF, NBA50): This lanky, red-headed center is considered by many to be the best college player ever. He headed the "Walton Gang" under *John Wooden* at *UCLA* that amassed an 88-game win streak (still a *record*) and won 2 *NCAA titles* (1972, 1973) as he was twice named *Final Four MVP*. Knee problems in H.S. forced him to develop his *rebounding* to start the *fast-break* that marked his teams' successes. His weak knees also cut short his NBA career but not before he led the league in *blocked shots* (3.25) and was named *Finals* MVP in leading the Portland Trailblazers to the championship in 1976-77. A cooperative, unselfish player, he is an intensely private, yet outspoken man of convictions. His political involvements in anti-war campus demonstrations in 1972 led to his arrest and the disapproval of his teammates. A big fan of The Grateful Dead since 1969, Walton has attended over 600 of their concerts, once played drums with them in Egypt, and still draws inspiration from an autographed poster wishing him well when he injured his foot as a player. Today he is one of the most popular and outspoken basketball analysts on TV.

WEST, JERRY (Guard, R, HF, NBA50): The NBA's logo of a basketball player is patterned after the left-handed West who joined the *L.A. Lakers* from West Virginia University for a career as one of the NBA's finest *guards*. Speed was his greatest asset and he got his graceful *jump shot* off faster and with more accuracy than anyone, as he averaged 27.0 *ppg* over his career (4th best all-time). Once he overcame his awe as a *rookie*, he unleashed a great *shooting touch* that was effective from anywhere on the floor. "Mr. Outside" made an explosive combination with *Elgin Baylor* on the *inside*. In 1969 he was NBA *Finals MVP* even though his team lost. It took 11 years before a 33-game winning streak (still a *record*) culminated in an NBA *title* (1972). That same year West led the league in *assists* and was voted *All-Star Game* MVP. West is also one of the shrewdest executives in the history of sports. He ran the Lakers for 19 years as general manger and executive vice-president, where his astute trades led to the championship teams of the '80s and '90s and the acquisitions of *Kobe Bryant* and *Shaquille O'Neal*. West retired from the Lakers in 2000, but barely one year later was wooed out of retirement by the challenge of building the Memphis Grizzlies as their President of Basketball Operations.

WOODEN, JOHN (Coach, R, HF): This 3-time All-American (1930-32) and National *Player of the Year* (1932) was a brilliant scorer and defensive player at Purdue. As *coach* at Indiana State (1946-48) and then *UCLA* (1949-1975), he collected 664 wins, still 7th all-time among *Division* I coaches. By following the principles of his *Pyramid of Success* (See **Fig. 28**) he led a UCLA program with no facilities, no winning tradition and no recruiting to 10 *NCAA titles* (a *record* to this day, the next best is 4). His dream was to coach in the Big 10 so he stalled in responding to a UCLA offer while hoping to receive one from Minnesota. When a snowstorm delayed the Minnesota offer an hour, he had accepted with UCLA and stuck to his word. The "Wizard of Westwood" originated the *full-court press* which revolutionized the game in the 1960s. He is one of only two individuals to be twice-honored by the *Hall of Fame*. Now in his 90s, he still sits in the corner bleachers of Pauley Pavilion during Bruin games, masking his emotions as carefully as ever.

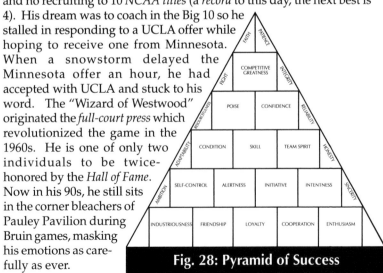

Fig. 28: Pyramid of Success

GLOSSARY

Please check the Index if you do not find what you are looking for here.

ABL (American Basketball League): a professional women's league created in 1996 that merged into the *WNBA* in 1998.

alive: a ball is alive when it is released by a *shooter* or thrower, or legally tapped by a jumper during a *jump* ball; the *game clock* starts only when the ball becomes alive; compare with *live*.

alternating-possession rule: in college, the *possession arrow* changes direction after each subsequent *jump ball* situation, alternating which team gets *possession* for the *throw-in*.

assist: the last *pass* to a teammate that leads directly to a *field goal*; the scorer must move immediately toward the *basket* for the passer to be credited with an assist; only 1 assist can be credited per field goal.

backboard: rectangular structure, 6' x 3 $\frac{1}{2}$', to which the *basket* is attached.

backcourt: the area from the *midcourt line* to the *end line* furthest from the *offense*'s *basket*.

ball handler: the player with the ball; usually the *point guard* at the start of a play.

bank shot: a *shot* where the ball is first bounced (or banked) off the *backboard* at such an angle that it then drops into the *basket*.

baseline: see *end line*.

basket: attached to the *backboard*, it consists of a metal *rim* 18" in diameter suspended 10' from the *floor*, from which a 15-18" corded *net* hangs, and through which *points* are scored; also refers to a successful *field goal*.

beat the defender: when an offensive player, with or without the ball, is able to get past an opponent who is *guarding* him.

bench: reserve players; those not included in the *starting lineup*.

blind pass: a *pass* from a *ball handler* who does not see his *receiver*, but is estimating where he should be.

blocked shot: the successful deflection of a *shot* by touching part of the ball on its way to the *basket*, thereby preventing a *field goal*.

blocking: the use of a defender's body position to illegally prevent an opponent's advance; the opposite of *charging*.

boosters: alumni supporters of college teams.

boxing out: a player's attempt to position his body between his opponents and the *basket* to get *rebounds* and prevent the opponents from doing so.

break: see *fast break*.

center circle: the circular area at *midcourt* from which *jump* balls are taken.

charging: an offensive *foul* which occurs when an offensive player runs into a defender who has *established position*.

Commissioner: the president of the *NBA*.

court: the 94' x 50' area bounded by 2 *sidelines* and 2 *end lines* containing a *basket* at each end, on which a basketball game is played.

court vision: a player's ability to see everything on the *court* during play — such as where his teammates and defenders are set up — which enables him to make better choices in *passing*; the best *point guards* possess this.

crossover dribble: when a *ball handler dribbles* the ball across his body from one hand to the other.

cylinder: the imaginary area directly above the *basket* where *goaltending* or *basket interference* can occur.

dead ball: any ball that is not *live*; occurs after each successful *field goal* or *free-throw* attempt, after any *official's* whistle or if the ball leaves the *court*; it stops play which is then resumed by a *jump* ball, *throw-in* or *free-throw*.

defense: the act of preventing the *offense* from scoring; the team without the ball.

defensive rebound: a *rebound* of an opponent's missed shot.

double-double (triple or quadruple-double): when a player scores double digits (10 or more) in 2 (3 or 4) categories during one game (*points, assists* and *rebounds* are most common, but it can also be *blocks* or *steals*); a rare accomplishment and a sign of great versatility.

double team: when two teammates join efforts in *guarding* a single opponent.

downcourt or down the court: the direction a team on *offense* moves, from its *backcourt* into its *frontcourt* and towards its own *basket*.

draft: the method by which *NBA* teams annually select college or *foreign players* to their teams, designed to promote balanced competition.

Dream Team: the name given by the media to the U.S. team that won the gold medal at the 1992 Barcelona Olympics; it was the first time non-amateurs were permitted to represent the country; the members of this team were *Charles Barkley, Larry Bird,* Clyde Drexler, Patrick Ewing, *Magic Johnson, Michael Jordan,* Christian Laettner, *Karl Malone,* Chris Mullin, *Scottie Pippen,* David Robinson and *John Stockton.* In the 1996 Olympics, the U.S. team was called Dream Team II and in 2000 Dream Team III.

dribble or dribbling: when a player repeatedly pushes, pats, taps or bats the ball toward the *floor* with one hand to cause it to bounce back up to either of his hands; used to advance the ball or keep control of it.

dribble series: a number of consecutive *dribbles* which end when a player allows the ball to rest in one or both hands; a player is only permitted one dribble series before he must *pass* or *shoot*.

drive to the basket: to move rapidly toward the *basket* with the ball.

dunk: when a player close to the *basket* jumps and strongly throws the ball down into it; an athletic, creative *shot* used to intimidate opponents.

elbowing: it is a *violation* if a player vigorously or excessively swings his elbows, even if there is no contact; it is a *foul* if contact is made, and an automatic ejection if that contact is above shoulder level.

end line: the boundary line behind each *basket*; also called the *baseline*.

established position: when a defensive player has both feet firmly planted on the *floor* before an offensive player's head and shoulder get past him; the offensive player who runs into such a defender is guilty of *charging*.

fake or feint: a deceptive move to throw a defender off balance and allow an offensive player to *shoot* or receive a *pass*; players use their eyes, head or any other part of the body to trick an opponent.

fast break: also called the run-and-shoot offense, generally it begins with a *defensive rebound* by a player who immediately sends an *outlet pass* toward *midcourt* to his waiting teammates who sprint to their *basket* and quickly *shoot* before enough opponents catch up to stop them.

field goal: when the ball enters the *basket* from above during play; worth 2 *points* (3 points if *shooter* was standing behind the *3-point line*).

Finals, NBA: the annual championship series of the *NBA's post-season*.

Final Four: the 4 regional champions (West, East, Midwest and Southeast) remaining from the 64 college teams that compete in the annual *NCAA Tournament*; they play one another to determine the national champion. There is a separate men's and women's tournament.

flagrant foul: unnecessary or excessive contact against an opponent; after it shoots *free-throws*, the fouled player's team also gets *possession* on a *throw-in*.

floor: the area of the *court* within the *end lines* and *sidelines*.

floor violation: a player's action that violates the rules but does not prevent an opponent's movement or cause him harm; penalized by a change in *possession*.

forwards: the 2 players on the *court* for a team who are usually smaller than the *center* and bigger than the *guards*; often a team's highest scorers.

foul: actions by players which break the rules but are not *floor violations*; penalized by a change in *possession* or *free-throw* opportunities; see *personal foul* or *technical foul*.

foul lane: the painted area 19' x 16' (12' in college and women's basketball) bordered by the *end line* and the *foul line*, outside which players must stand during a *free-throw*; also the area an offensive player cannot spend more than *3-seconds* at a time in.

foul line: the line 15' from the *backboard* and parallel to the *end line* from which players shoot *free-throws*.

foul shot: see *free-throw*.

foul trouble: when a player is close to being ejected from the game for commiting too many *personal fouls*.

4-point play: a *3-point shot* followed by a successful *free-throw*.

franchise: a professional team.

franchise player: a star player around which a *franchise* is built.

free agent, restricted: an NBA player whose contract has expired and who has received a "qualifying offer" from his current club which provides a salary level predetermined by the *collective bargaining agreement*. While this player is free to negotiate an offer from a new team, his current team has a *right of first refusal* to match that offer, thereby obligating him to remain with his current team.

free agent, unrestricted: a player who has completed his 3rd NBA season (or 4th season, if his current team exercised its "option" to have him play for a 4th year) and is free to negotiate a contract with other NBA teams without his current team having a *right of first refusal*.

free-throw: an un*guard*ed shot worth 1 *point* taken from the *foul line* by a player whose opponent committed a *personal* or *technical foul*.

free-throw line: see *foul line*.

free-throw line extended: an imaginary line drawn from the *free-throw* line to the *sideline* to determine the location for certain *throw-ins*.

frontcourt: the area between the *midcourt line* and the *end line* closest to the *offense*'s *basket*.

full-court press: when defenders start *guarding* the *offense* in its *backcourt*.

game clock: shows how much time remains in each of the four 12-minute *quarters* of an *NBA* game or the two 20-minute *halves* of a college or *WNBA* game.

guards: the two players on each team who are the smallest on the *court*; they usually handle setting up plays and *passing* to teammates closer to the *basket*.

guarding: the act of following an opponent around the *court* to prevent him from getting close to the *basket*, taking an *open shot* or making an easy *pass*, while avoiding illegal contact.

half-court or set offense: when a team takes the time to develop a play in its *frontcourt* (e.g., *give-and-go* or a *screening play*); opposite of *fast break*.

high percentage shot: a *shot* that is likely to go in the *basket*, such as a *layup*.

high post: an imaginary area outside either side of the *foul lane* at the *free-throw line extended*.

illegal defense: a violation in the NBA that used to be called against a team for using a *zone defense* when playing zone was illegal (1961-2001); a team received a simple warning for its 1st offense in a game, but a *technical foul* was called against it for each subsequent offense.

in the paint: being in the *foul lane* area which is painted a different color.

in the penalty: see *over the limit*.

inbounds: the area within the *end lines* and *sidelines* of the *court*; also the act of bringing the ball into this area by means of a *throw-in*.

incidental contact: minor contact that does not affect the outcome of a play usually overlooked by *officials*.

inside shooting: *shots* taken by a player near or under the *basket*.

jump ball: 2 opposing players jump for a ball an *official* tosses above and between them, each trying to tap it to his teammates to gain *possession*; used to start the game (*tip-off*) and *overtime periods*, and sometimes to *restart* play.

keepaway game: a tactic used by the team that is leading near the end of the game to keep the ball from its opponents to prevent them from scoring while using up time off the *game clock*; also called *freezing*.

key or keyhole: the area at each end of the *court* consisting of the *foul circle*, *foul lane* and *free-throw line*; named for the shape it had years ago.

layup or layin: a shot taken after *driving to the basket* by leaping up under the *basket* and using one hand to drop the ball directly into the basket (layin) or to *bank* the ball off the *backboard* into it (layup).

leading the receiver: when a *passer* throws the ball where he thinks a *receiver* is headed.

live ball: as soon as a ball is given to a *free-throw shooter* or a *thrower* on a *throw-in*, it is live, but the *game clock* does not restart until the ball is *alive*.

lockout: a work stoppage imposed by NBA team owners during which teams may not negotiate player contracts, sign *free agents* or make *trades*; a tactic used to pressure the *Players' Association* (union) in *collective bargaining agreement* negotiations.

loose ball: a ball that is *alive* but not in the *possession* of either team.

low post: an imaginary area outside either side of the *foul lane* close to the *basket*.

lower percentage shot: a *shot* that is less likely to go in the *basket*, such as one thrown by a player who is off balance or outside his *shooting range*.

man-to-man defense: the defensive style where each defensive player is responsible for *guarding* one opponent.

March Madness: see *NCAA Tournament*.

match-ups: any pairing of players on opposing teams who *guard* each other.

MVP (Most Valuable Player): an award recognizing the *NBA* player who contributed most to his team during the *regular season* or the *Finals*.

NBA (National Basketball Association): a professional league created in 1949 that now has 29 teams, 1 of which is in Canada.

NCAA (National Collegiate Athletic Association): a voluntary association of over 1,200 colleges and universities in the U.S. whose role is to establish standards and protect the integrity of amateurism for student-athletes.

NCAA Tournament: an annual competition between 64 college teams to crown a national champion; also called *March Madness* because the three-week-long event is held during March; see also *Final Four*.

NIT (National Invitational Tournament): the oldest college tournament, in which 32 teams not selected to the *NCAA Tournament* compete each year.

off the dribble: a *shot* taken while *driving to the basket*.

offense: the team with *possession* of the ball.

offensive rebound: a *rebound* of a team's own missed shot.

officials: the *crew chief*, *referee(s)* and *umpire(s)* who control the game, stop and start play, and impose penalties for *violations* and *fouls*.

1-and-1 or 1-plus-1: in college, a *free-throw* attempt that earns the *shooter* a 2nd attempt only <u>if</u> the first is successful.

open: when a player is un*guard*ed by a defender.

out of bounds: the area outside of and including the *end lines* and *sidelines*.

outside shooting: *shots* taken from the *perimeter*.

over the limit: when a team commits 5 or more *team fouls* per *NBA period* (4 in each *overtime*); 8 or more per *WNBA* half; 7 or more per *half* in college; this team is also said to be *in the penalty*.

overtime or OT: the extra *period*(s) played after a *regulation game* ends tied.

pass: when a player throws the ball to a teammate; used to *start* plays, move the ball *downcourt*, keep it away from defenders and get it to a *shooter*.

passer: the player who *passes* the ball to a teammate.

period: any *quarter, half* or *overtime* segment.

perimeter: the area beyond the *foul circle* away from the *basket*, including the *3-point line*, from which players take long-range shots.

personal foul: contact between players that may result in *injury* or provide one team with an unfair advantage; players may not *push, hold,* trip, hack, *elbow,* restrain or *charge* into an opponent; these are also counted as *team fouls*.

picked off: refers to a defender who has been successfully prevented from reaching the *ball handler* by an offensive *screen*.

pick-up games: impromptu games played among players who just met.

pivot: a *center*; also the foot that must remain touching the *floor* until a *ball handler* who has stopped *dribbling* is ready to *pass* or *shoot*.

playmaker: the *point guard* who generally sets up plays for his teammates.

point-shaving: an illegal practice where players intentionally win a game, but by fewer *points* than the *point spread*; led to 2 major college scandals (involved 32 of the biggest stars in the 1950s, then 22 colleges in 1961).

point spread: a device established by bookmakers to equalize 2 teams for betting purposes; e.g., if a team is considered to be 4 points better than another, the spread is 4 points; to win a bet on the favorite, that team would need to win by more than the spread (in this case, by more than 4 points); the margin of victory can be more important than whether a team wins or loses.

possession: to be holding or in control of the ball.

possession arrow: used in college, to determine which team's turn it is to *inbound* the ball to begin a *period* or in a *jump ball* situation.

post position: the position of a player standing in the *low* or *high post*.

rebound: when a player grabs a ball that is coming off the *rim* or *backboard* after a missed *shot*; see *offensive rebound* and *defensive rebound*.

receiver: the player who receives a *pass* from the *ball handler*.

regulation game: four 12-minute *quarters* in the *NBA* or two 20-minute *halves* in college or the *WNBA*; a game that ends without *overtime periods*.

release: the moment that the ball leaves a *shooter's* hands.

right of first refusal: the right of a *restricted free agent's* current team to match the terms negotiated between the player and a new team, thereby obligating the player to remain with his current team.

rookie: a player in his first *NBA* season.

roster: the list of players on a team.

run: occurs when one team scores several *field goals* in quick succession while its opponents score few or none.

salary cap: an annual dollar limit that a single team may pay all its players collectively.

scoring opportunity: when a player gets *open* for a *shot* that he is likely to make.

screen or screener: the offensive player who stands between a teammate and a defender to give his teammate the chance to take an *open shot*.

shot clock: a clock that limits the time a team with the ball has to shoot it; *24 seconds* in the *NBA* and 30 seconds in the *WNBA*; in college, *35 seconds* for men, *30 seconds* for women.

shooter: a player who takes a *shot* at the *basket*.

shooter's roll: the ability to get even an inaccurate *shot* to bounce lightly off the *rim* and into the *basket*.

shooting range: the distance from which a player is likely to make his *shots*.

sidelines: 2 boundary lines that run the length of the *court*.

sixth man: the best *substitute* on a team; usually the first player to come off the *bench* to replace a *starter*.

slam dunk: see *dunk*.

squaring up: when a player's shoulders are facing the *basket* as he *releases* the ball for a *shot*; considered good shooting position.

starting lineup: the 5 *starters* who begin a game; usually a team's best players.

substitute: a player who joins the game to replace a player on the *court*.

swing man: a player who can play both the *guard* and *forward* positions.

team fouls: each *personal foul* committed by a player is also counted against his team; when a team goes *over the limit*, its opponent is awarded *free-throw* opportunities.

technical fouls or "Ts": procedural violations and misconduct that *officials* believe are detrimental to the game; penalized by the non-offending team shooting a *free-throw* (2 free-throws and *possession* in college).

3-on-3: a game played with only 3 players on the *court* for each team.

3-point play: a 2-point *field goal* followed by a successful *free-throw*.

3-point shot: a *field goal* worth 3 points because the *shooter* had both feet (or one foot if the other is in mid-air) behind the *3-point line* prior to *releasing* the ball.

throw-in: the method by which a team with *possession inbounds* the ball.

timeout: when play is temporarily suspended by an *official* or at the request of a team to respond to an injured player or discuss strategy; there are *full timeouts* (100 or 60 seconds in *NBA*, 120 seconds in *WNBA*, 75 or 60 seconds in college) and *20-second timeouts* (30 seconds in college).

tip-off: the initial *jump* ball that starts the game.

title: a championship.

transition: the shift from *offense* to *defense*, or defense to offense.

traveling: a *floor violation* when the *ball handler* takes too many steps without dribbling; also called walking.

turnover: when the *offense* loses *possession* through its own fault by committing a *floor violation*, or by passing the ball *out of bounds* or to an opponent.

up-and-down violation: a form of *traveling*, where a player attempting a *jump shot* lands before *releasing* the ball.

upset: when a lower-*seeded* (inferior) team beats a higher-seeded (superior) one.

violation: see *floor violation*.

weakside: the side of the *court* away from the ball.

WNBA (Women's National Basketball Association): a professional women's league created in 1997 affiliated with the *NBA*.

zone defense: a defense where each *defender* is responsible for an area of the *court* and must *guard* any player who enters that area; compare with *man-to-man* defense.

119

INDEX

Bolded page numbers indicate a photograph, diagram or table.

121

OFFICIALS' HAND SIGNALS

TIME IN: chopping motion with a hand or finger.

TIMEOUT or **STOP CLOCK**: arm raised with open palm facing out. (See p. 20-24)

20-SECOND TIME-OUT: both hands touching shoulders. (See p. 21-22)

DIRECTION OF PLAY: arm outstretched in front of the body with a finger pointing in the direction while the color of the team going on offense is called.

JUMP BALL: thumbs of both hands raised above the head. (See p. 15-17)

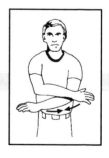

CANCEL SCORE, CANCEL PLAY or **NO SCORE**: outstretched arms crossed then uncrossed in front of the body.

3-POINT FIELD GOAL: one arm is raised above the head when an attempt is made, and the other is raised if the shot is successful. (See p. 11)

PERSONAL FOUL: clenched fist raised above the head. (See p.49-53)

DOUBLE FOUL: clenched fists waved across each other above the head. (See p. 55)

TECHNICAL FOUL: both hands used to form the letter "T" at chest level. (See p. 53-54)

LOOSE BALL FOUL: both arms extended to the side at shoulder level. (See p. 52)

TO DESIGNATE AN OFFENDER: fingers held up to indicate the player's jersey number (each hand represents one digit). (See p. 40)

BASKET INTERFERENCE: finger of one hand rotated around a fist formed by the other hand in front of the body. (See p. 49)

GOALTENDING: 2 fingers waved downward to indicate 2 points are being awarded to the offense. (See p. 48-49)

3-SECOND RULE VIOLATION (OFFENSIVE OR DEFENSIVE): 3 fingers held up in the air. (See p. 47)

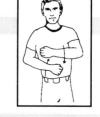

TRAVELING: two clenched fists and forearms rotated around each other in front of the body. (See p. 48)

24-SECOND VIOLATION: top of the head tapped with an open palm. (See p. 48)

BLOCKING: both hands placed on the hips. (See p. 51)

CHARGING: clenched fist with the arm outstretched to the side at shoulder level. (See p. 51)

HOLDING: one wrist grabbed with the opposite hand. (See p. 53)

ILLEGAL FOREARM: one arm folded at chest level extended parallel to the floor. (See p. 52)

ILLEGAL DRIBBLE or **DOUBLE DRIBBLE**: patting motion in front of the body with one hand at a time. (See p. 45)

ILLEGAL SCREEN OUT OF BOUNDS: arms crossed at chest level. (See p.48)

ILLEGAL USE OF HANDS: forearm area struck with the pinky side of the opposite hand.

PUSHING: pushing motion with both palms facing out from the chest. (See p. 53)

127

ORDER FORM

Order any of the following Spectator Guides:

Title	Qty	Price	Total
Basketball Made Simple, 3rd ed.		$11.95	
Football Made Simple, 4th ed.		$11.95	
Ice Hockey Made Simple, 4th ed.		$11.95	
Soccer Made Simple		$11.95	
How To Win a Sports Scholarship, 2nd ed.		$19.95	

Subtotal		
Add $2.99 plus $0.99 per book for shipping & handling → S&H		
Sales Tax (in CA only)		
Total		

Order by phone toll-free: **(800) 247-8228** or (310) 318-3006

Order on the Internet at: **www.firstbasesports.com**

or

Mail this form to :   First Base Sports, Inc.
P.O. Box 1731
Manhattan Beach, CA 90267-1731

Name _____

Street Address _____

City _____

State _____   Zip _____

Phone No. _____

Method of Payment:

Check or M.O. ❑ or Credit Card: VISA ❑   MasterCard ❑

Card # _____ Exp. Date (required) _____

Signature _____ B/02